science

The Salters' Approach
Key Stage 4   Book 4

Bob Campbell   John Lazonby   Robin Millar   Steve Smyth

HEINEMANN EDUCATIONAL

The authors and publishers are grateful to the following for permission to reproduce photographs:

Contents:
T ESA/PLI/SPL, BL A.A. Riley/FLPA, ML Gray Mortimore/Allsport, MR British Gas, B National Power.

The Earth in Space:
p1 NASA/SPL; p3 NASA/SPL; p4 Steve Smyth; p8–9 NASA/SPL × 8, Earth ESA/PLI/SPL; p10 T NASA/SPL × 2, B J. Allan Cash × 2; p11 Andrew Lambert; p12 T Andrew Lambert, B Kodansha; p13 NASA/SPL; p16 L Royal Observatory Edinburgh, R Radio Astronomy Group, University of Cambridge.

Evolution:
p19 TL Gérard Lacz/NHPA, ML Hans Dieter Brand/FLPA, TR B.S. Turner/FLPA, MR Gérard Lacz/NHPA, BR Mark Newman/FLPA; p20 T Trevor Hill/Courtesy Stanley Gibbons, M Mary Evans; p21 Ann Ronan Picture Library × 2; p24 Nigel Cattlin/Holt Studios Ltd; p25 Ann Ronan Picture Library; p26 A. A. Riley/FLPA; p27 Julia Kamlish/SPL; p28 TL Richard Anthony/Holt Studios Ltd, BL Natural History Museum, TR Nigel Cattlin/Holt Studios Ltd, MR Ray F. Bird/FLPA, BR Dept of Clin. Cytogenetics, Addenbrookes Hospital, Cambridge/SPL; p29 T J. Allan Cash, B Zefa; p33 A.C. Barrington-Brown, Courtesy of Weidenfold; p34 L Shorthorn Society, R Nigel Cattlin/Holt Studios Ltd.

Heinemann Educational, a division of

Heinemann Educational Books Ltd
Halley Court, Jordan Hill, Oxford OX2 8EJ

OXFORD LONDON EDINBURGH MADRID
ATHENS BOLOGNA PARIS MELBOURNE
SYDNEY AUCKLAND SINGAPORE
TOKYO IBADAN NAIROBI HARARE
GABORONE PORTSMOUTH NH (USA)

ISBN 0 435 63011 3

First published 1992

92 93 94 95 96 11 10 9 8 7 6 5 4 3 2

©University of York Science Education Group

Designed and typeset by KAG Design Limited
Printed in Spain by Mateu Cromo

Sports Science:
p35 TL Tony Duffy/Allsport, M Gray Mortimore/Allsport, B Trevor Hill; p36 TL Sporting Pictures, TR Associated Sports Photography, BL Popperfoto, BR Gray Mortimore/Allsport; p37 Sporting Pictures; p40 T Allsport, TM Sporting Pictures, BM Sally & Richard Greenhill, B IBM; p42 T Associated Sports Photography, M Sporting Pictures; p43 T Sally & Richard Greenhill, B Steve Smyth; p44 L Steve Smyth, R Chemistry Photographics, University of York; p46 L Courtesy of The British Commercial Vehicle Museum, Leyland, R Children's World.

Burning and Bonding:
p49 T Zefa, B British Gas; p50 Ann Ronan Picture Library × 2; p51 T Ann Ronan Picture Library, B Royal Institution; p52 Sally & Richard Greenhill; p53 Ford Motor Company; p56 British Gas; p60 Ann Ronan Picture Library; p61 T Chemistry Photographics, University of York, B Associated Octel Co. Ltd; p64 Trevor Hill; p65 Trevor Hill.

Energy Today and Tomorrow:
p67 TL AEA Technology, TR Trevor Hill, M Steve Smyth, BL Trevor Hill; pp68–9 Bryan Milner; p72 National Power; p73 T Southern Electric, ML Southern Electric, MR Trevor Hill, BL National Power, B Steve Smyth; p76 Zefa; p78 National Power; p79 National Power; p80 AEA Technology; p81 AEA Technology × 2; p83 TL Tony Morrison/South American Pictures, B Zefa, TR ETSU; p84 National Power; p85 JET Joint Undertaking.

(T = Top; B = Bottom; R = Right; L = Left; M = Middle)
Picture research by Jennifer Johnson.

We are indebted to many companies and institutions for their encouragement and financial assistance; in particular, to BP, Heinemann Educational Books, ICI, the Salters' Institute of Industrial Chemistry, and the Training, Enterprise and Educational Directorate.

About this book

Salters' Science 4 is different from conventional textbooks, so read this section carefully to find out how to use it. (It's not just a case of reading each chapter from beginning to end!)

This textbook accompanies the 18th - 22nd units of the Salters' Course at Key Stage 4. These five units are:

- The Earth In Space
- Evolution
- Sports Science
- Burning and Bonding
- Energy Today and Tomorrow

Each unit has a corresponding chapter in this book.

Each chapter is divided into five key sections.

- Introducing
- Looking At
- In Brief
- Thinking About
- Things to do

These sections are meant to be used in different ways. Have a quick look at a chapter to see what each section is like and then turn back to this page and read about how to use them.

Introducing

This page sets the scene and tells you why the topic is important and what the chapter covers.

You could read this page before you start to study the topic in class.

Looking at

There are several Looking At pages in each chapter. Each page uses coloured photographs and diagrams to show an important application or use of the science ideas. The page sets you tasks to help you to understand these ideas.

Your teacher will ask you to work through some Looking At pages and to do the tasks on the page.

In brief

This section presents a summary of what you need to know and understand about the topic.

You could use the In Brief when you have finished a unit or when you are revising. Key ideas from this section are explained more fully in the next section.

Thinking about

This explains the key scientific ideas developed in the unit.

When revising, you might find a part of the In Brief that you need to do more work on. You can then move to the Thinking About to find out more about it. Your teacher might ask you to read parts of this section after you have met the ideas in class.

Things to do

This is a collection of things for you to do. There are:
- Activities to try
- Things to find out
- Things to write about
- Points to discuss
- Questions to answer

You could use a selection of these either in class or for homework.

Contents

THE EARTH IN SPACE — 1

Introducing *The Earth in space* 1
Looking at *The Earth in space* 2
The flight of *Apollo 11* 2
Tides 4
In brief *The Earth in space* 6
Thinking about *The Earth in space* 8
1 How did the solar system form? 8
2 How can we travel in space? 10
3 What happens when a spacecraft lifts off? 11
4 How are spacecraft able to stay in orbit around the Earth? 12
5 What keeps things moving in a circle? 13
6 Weight and mass: what's the difference? 14
7 How do we know about the Universe? 15
Things to do 18

EVOLUTION — 19

Introducing *Evolution* 19
Looking at *Evolution* 20
The work of Darwin and Wallace 20
Fossils 22
Peas in a pod 24
In brief *Evolution* 26
Thinking about *Evolution* 28
1 What is natural selection? 28
2 What is artificial selection? 28
3 Why are chromosomes important? 28
4 How can we predict patterns of inheritance? 30
5 Male or female? 31
6 Why are more males colour blind than females? 31
7 What is the genetic code? 31
8 What is genetic engineering? 32
Things to do 33

SPORTS SCIENCE 35

Introducing *Sports science*	35
Looking at *Sports science*	36
Jumping and vaulting	36
In brief *Sports science*	38
Thinking about *Sports science*	40
1 What is work?	40
2 How powerful are you?	41
3 What is fitness?	41
4 What causes the changes in your body after exercise?	42
5 How can we calculate amounts of kinetic energy and potential energy?	42
6 How can we use the potential energy and kinetic energy equations?	43
7 How do people move?	43
8 How do things balance?	45
Things to do	46

BURNING AND BONDING 49

Introducing *Burning and bonding* 49
Looking at *Burning and bonding* 50
Sir Humphrey Davy 50
Cars and air pollution 52
In brief *Burning and bonding* 54
Thinking about *Burning and bonding* 56
1 What happens when a hydrocarbon fuel burns? 56
2 How do atoms in compounds stick together? 58
3 How does the periodic table explain the properties of elements? 60
4 How can we explain the patterns in the periodic table? 62
5 How do atoms in elements stick together? 64
Things to do 65

ENERGY TODAY AND TOMORROW 67

Introducing *Energy today and tomorrow* 67
Looking at *Energy today and tomorrow* 68
Energy self-sufficiency 68
Dealing with the waste 70
The National Grid 72
In brief *Energy today and tomorrow* 74
Thinking about *Energy today and tomorrow* 76
1 What do we use fuels for? 76
2 How do we make electricity? 77
3 How does a power station work? 78
4 How do we use nuclear fuel? 80
5 What are renewable energy sources? 82

6 Nuclear fusion – unlimited energy for the future? 85
7 How can we change voltages? 85
Things to do 87

Index 89

Introducing

THE EARTH IN SPACE

THE EARTH IN SPACE 1

The Earth is a small planet, moving in an almost circular path around the Sun. Along with eight other planets and some smaller objects, it forms the **solar system** of bodies held by the Sun's gravitational field. The Sun is an average sized star lying in one of the arms of a spiral **galaxy** called the Milky Way. The Milky Way galaxy contains at least 100 000 million stars. It is one of a group of about 20 'local' galaxies. There are thought to be thousands of millions of galaxies in the Universe, many of them much larger than the Milky Way.

The Earth is just the right size and the right distance from the Sun to have an atmosphere of oxygen and nitrogen, and an average surface temperature at which the chemical compound water (H_2O) is liquid. Its crust contains the element carbon, which can form very many different compounds, including some on which life depends. There may be other planets in the Universe with conditions suitable to support life, but at present we do not know of any.

This famous photograph is called Earthrise:

1. Where is the Earth in the photograph?
2. What is the surface that the space vehicle is moving above?
3. Where do you think this photograph was taken from?
4. Why is only part of the Earth visible?
5. Why does the Earth have the colours shown in the photograph?

IN THIS CHAPTER YOU WILL FIND OUT
- about the solar system and some theories about how it was formed
- about rockets and how they move
- about the motion of projectiles
- about the gravitational force and the role it plays in the motion of the planets, satellites and spacecraft
- about weight and mass and how they differ
- how some important discoveries about the Universe were made.

Looking at

The Flight of Apollo 11

LOOKING AT: THE EARTH IN SPACE

The flight of *Apollo 11* is probably the most famous space flight ever. It was the mission that first landed a person on the Moon. This diagram shows some of the important stages on the journey.

1 Lift-off from Cape Canaveral. Enormous first stage rockets were required here to provide sufficient thrust to lift the rocket against the pull of Earth's gravity.

2 Once the craft was away from the Earth's surface the first stage was no longer required. It separated from the rest of the craft and was abandoned.

3 At this point the craft was moving around the Earth. With no air resistance to slow it down, the craft kept a constant speed. The effect of the Earth's gravity was to keep the craft in orbit.

4 To move away from Earth orbit required a force. This was provided by igniting the engine at a point calculated to take the craft towards the Moon.

5 Once on course for the Moon the engine was only required to change direction.

15 ...to splash down in the Pacific Ocean.

14 Moving more slowly, the command module spiralled down towards the Earth...

13 At this point, all of the craft apart from the command module was abandoned.

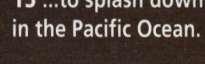

1. Make a list of headings for each of the main stages of the *Apollo 11* flight. Arrange these headings in sequence to make a flow diagram.
2. Beside each stage on your flow diagram, write a short note describing the size of the force exerted by *Apollo 11*'s rocket motors at this stage. Use words like large, small, no force, etc.
3. Choose one point where the force exerted by the rocket motors was large. Explain why a large force was needed at this point. Choose another point where the force exerted by the rocket motors was small, or zero. Explain why only a small force or no force at all was needed at this point.
4. At one point on both the outward and the return journey, the gravitational pull of the Earth on the spacecraft was exactly balanced by the gravitational pull of the Moon. Draw a sketch diagram and mark on it roughly where you think this point would be. Explain the reasons for your answer. Would it be true to say that, at this point, the spacecraft was in a region of zero gravitational field?
5. The lunar module has much less powerful motors than the *Saturn* rockets which lifted *Apollo 11* off the Earth. It is also much less streamlined in shape than the *Saturn* rocket. Explain why the lunar module could be designed in this way.

LOOKING AT: THE EARTH IN SPACE 3

John W. Young on the Moon's surface in 1972. He was Commander of the *Apollo 16* flight which was launched in 1972, three years after *Apollo 11*.

6 When the craft was close to the Moon, the Moon's gravity kept the craft in orbit, at a constant speed.

7 Here the lunar module separated from the rest of the craft. Moving slowly, the lunar module began to spiral down towards the Moon.

8 The lunar module's engine was switched on in reverse. The thrust from the engine was sufficient to slow the descent to the Moon, but not enough to overcome the gravitational attraction.

9 Landing! The astronauts spent $21\frac{1}{2}$ hours on the surface of the Moon.

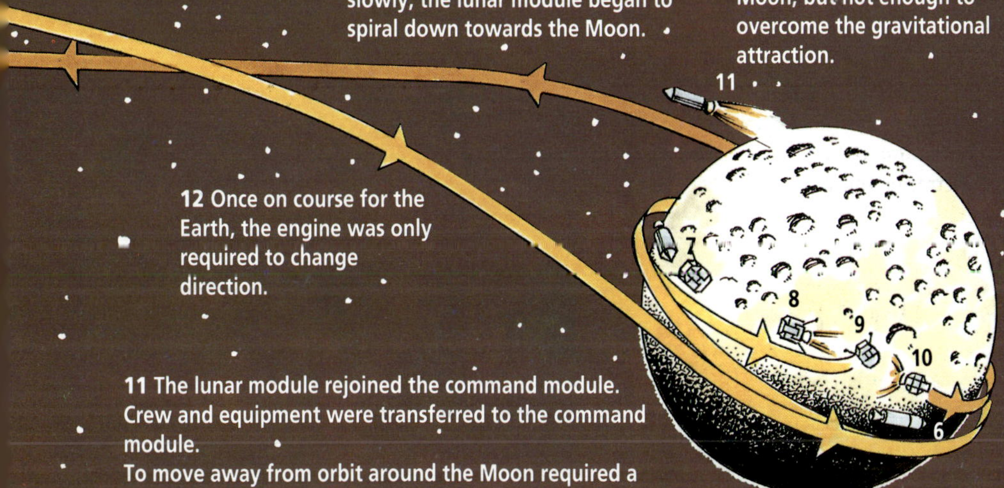

12 Once on course for the Earth, the engine was only required to change direction.

11 The lunar module rejoined the command module. Crew and equipment were transferred to the command module.
To move away from orbit around the Moon required a force. This was provided by igniting the engine at a point calculated to take the craft towards the Earth.

10 Take-off from the Moon. The lunar module's engines now had to provide sufficient thrust to lift it off the Moon. A much smaller force was required than on Earth, because the Moon's gravity is six times weaker.

Looking at

Tides

LOOKING AT: THE EARTH IN SPACE

Have you ever been lying on a beach and had to move because the tide was coming in? Do you know anywhere that is cut off by an incoming tide?

High tide and low tide at South Bay, Scarborough

What causes tides?

Tides on Earth are caused mainly by the Moon, though the Sun also has an effect. This diagram shows a simplified model in which the Earth is completely covered with water.

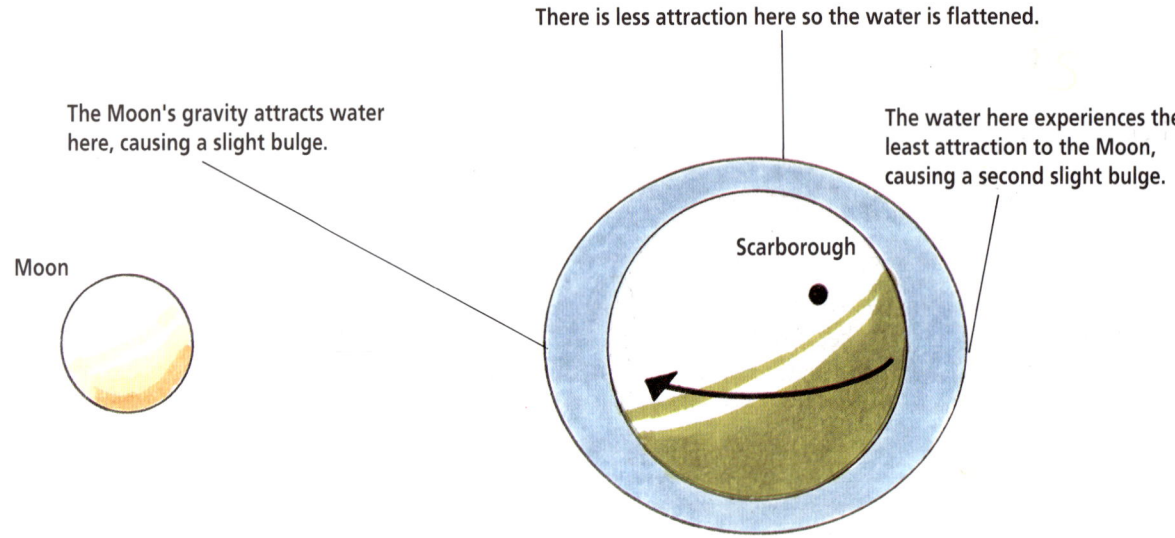

There is less attraction here so the water is flattened.

The Moon's gravity attracts water here, causing a slight bulge.

The water here experiences the least attraction to the Moon, causing a second slight bulge.

Moon

Scarborough

A point on the Earth, such as Scarborough, passes through both bulges each time the Earth rotates on its axis, giving two high tides each day.
But as the Moon moves around the Earth, the positions of the bulges move, so it actually takes slightly longer than 24 hours for Scarborough to pass through both bulges. The time between successive high tides is approximately 13 hours.

LOOKING AT: THE EARTH IN SPACE

The effect of the Sun
The Sun's effect on the tides is not nearly as great as the Moon's. It can be seen most readily when the Sun's gravity reinforces the Moon's:

(Distances not to scale)

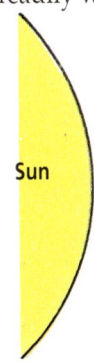

The Sun's gravitational force reinforces the Moon's, causing a larger bulge.

Tides are greater at this time of the month, and are known as **spring tides**. High tides are higher and low tides are lower.

At other times the Sun's effect opposes the Moon's.

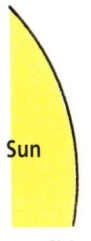

The Sun's gravitational force now acts against the Moon's. Tides are smaller at this time of the month, and are known as **neap tides**. High and low tides are less extreme.

The complete picture
This picture of tides is very simplified. The real situation is complicated by the fact that the Earth's surface is very irregular. The oceans have different depths and the coastlines have complicated shapes. Water cannot flow to give the simple bulges shown in the diagrams because the continents and islands get in the way.

These factors make tides very complicated. Some parts of the world have enormous rises and falls of water. The largest tidal difference, 18 m, is in the Bay of Fundy in Canada. In other places the tides are very small. The Mediterranean Sea has only a narrow connection with the rest of the world's oceans and is virtually tideless as a result.

Other strange tidal effects are caused by islands and the shapes of river mouths. Southampton has double tides because of the flow of the water around the Isle of Wight. The rivers Severn and Trent have **tidal bores** – waves of water that sweep along the river caused by the funnelling effect of water in their estuaries.

1. Draw another diagram showing a different position of the Moon that will cause a spring tide.
2. Draw another diagram showing a different position of the Moon that will cause a neap tide.
3. Which phases of the Moon bring spring tides? (What would the Moon look like from Earth in the top diagram?)
4. Which phases of the Moon bring neap tides? (Again, how would the Moon look in the second diagram?)
5. How would you measure the tidal difference at South Bay, Scarborough? How do you think it would compare with that at the Bay of Fundy?
6. What advantage does Southampton have as a port? Explain your answer.
7. Find out which rivers in other parts of the world have tidal bores.

In brief

The Earth in Space

1. The **solar system** consists of nine **planets**, and a belt of smaller bodies called **asteroids**, orbiting the Sun. **Comets** also orbit the Sun and are part of the solar system.

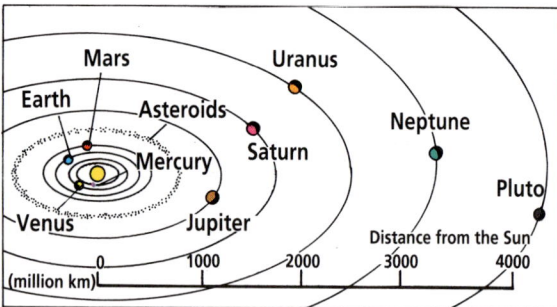

The planets' orbits round the Sun

The orbits of the planets are ellipses which are almost circular. Some planets have their own satellites or **moons** which orbit the planet.

2. We can see some patterns in the solar system:
   - all the planets orbit in the same plane
   - the surface temperatures of the planets get lower the further they are from the Sun
   - the larger planets (Jupiter, Saturn, Uranus and Neptune) are made mainly of substances with low melting points
   - the smaller planets are rocky.

3. These observations, along with others, suggest that the solar system formed from a single **nebula**, an enormous swirling cloud of dust and gas. The gravitational attraction between the particles of matter pulled them together to form the Sun and the planets.

4. The Sun is a **star**. Its fuel is hydrogen. In a process called **nuclear fusion**, hydrogen nuclei join together to make helium nuclei, releasing energy. All stars are powered by nuclear fusion.

5. When a star's fuel runs out, the star may collapse. The gravitational attraction between different parts of the star's matter pulls them all closer and closer together. The matter contracts to a very small dense centre, which may become a **white dwarf star**, a **neutron star** or a **black hole**.

6. The first stage of **space travel** is lift-off from the Earth. Because of the gravitational pull of the Earth, very large forces are needed to accelerate a rocket upwards. It has to reach a speed of 11 km/s or it will eventually fall back to Earth.

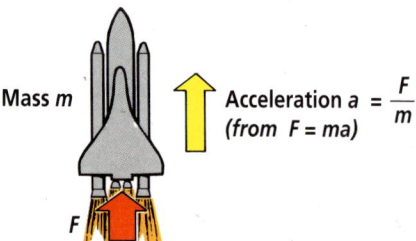

7. A spacecraft in deep space, far away from all planets or stars, moves at a steady speed in a straight line when its rocket motors are turned off. This is an example of Newton's first law of motion. A spacecraft in Earth orbit also continues to move at a steady speed without any rocket force.

8. In order to move, an object needs something to push back on. A rocket in space pushes on its own fuel. The backwards push of the rocket on the exhaust gases causes an equal and opposite forwards push on the rocket itself.

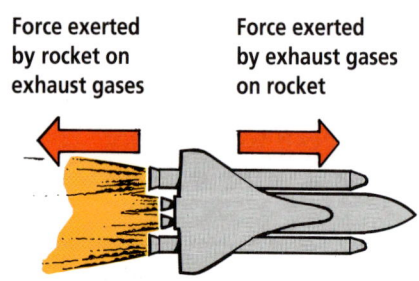

9. An object thrown vertically upwards slows down steadily until it reaches the top of its motion.
   On the way down, it speeds up again.

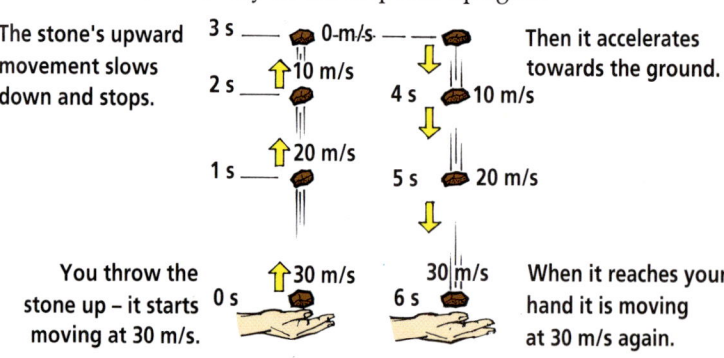

IN BRIEF: THE EARTH IN SPACE

10 An object projected forwards falls downwards at exactly the same rate as a free-falling object, provided air resistance can be ignored. The forwards motion makes no difference to how fast it drops.

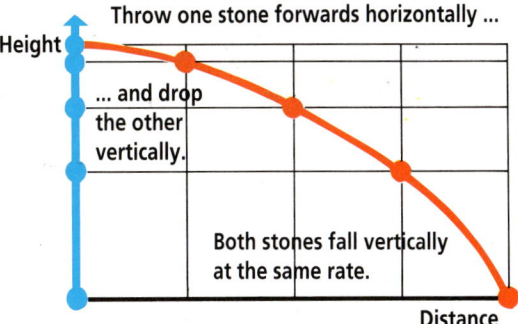

11 Because the Earth is a sphere, an object projected forwards at a high speed may fall towards the Earth at exactly the same rate as the Earth's surface curves away below it! It will continue moving round the Earth, falling towards it all the time, but never getting there. It has become a satellite in orbit.

12 An object can move in a circle only if there is a force pulling it towards the centre. Without such a force it will fly off in a straight line in the direction it was travelling when the force stopped acting on it.

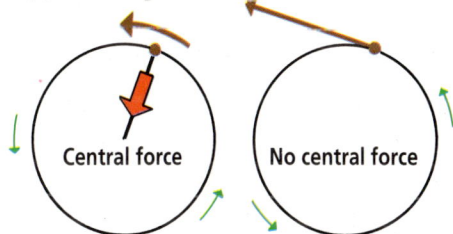

13 The force which keeps the Moon and artificial satellites in orbit around the Earth is the Earth's **gravitational force**. The Sun's gravitational force keeps the planets in their orbits around the Sun.

14 Every object exerts a gravitational force on every other object. This force is always an attraction. The greater the mass of the objects, the bigger the gravitational force. The gravitational force gets smaller as the distance between the two objects increases, but it never becomes zero.

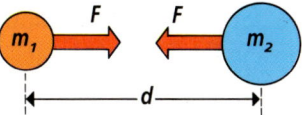

F increases as m_1 and m_2 increase.
F decreases as d increases.

15 The **weight** of an object (in newtons) is the size of the gravitational force on the object. This depends on where the object is. The **mass** of an object (in kilograms) is a measure of how much force is needed to make the object accelerate – its **inertia**. The mass of an object never changes, no matter where the object is. But the object's weight changes if you take it up a mountain or into space because the gravitational force on it changes.

16 At the Earth's surface, the strength of the gravitational field is roughly 10 N/kg. So a mass of 1 kg has a weight of about 10 N.
On the Moon, the gravitational field strength is 1.6 N/kg, so a kilogram will weigh 1.6 N. But it would be just as difficult to make the kilogram speed up on the Moon as on Earth.

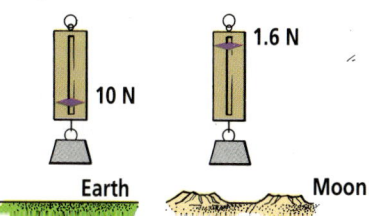

17 Our knowledge of the Universe is based on **observation**. Scientists develop **theories** to explain what they observe. Sometimes these theories can be used to make exact **predictions**. If **new observations** agree with the predictions, this makes us more confident in the theory.
Other advances in astronomy have come from new observations which could *not* be explained by the theories available at the time. This led to the development of new and more powerful theories.

Thinking about
The Earth in Space

THINKING ABOUT: THE EARTH IN SPACE

1. How did the solar system form?

It is thought that the solar system was formed about a thousand million years ago, from an enormous cloud of hydrogen and helium. These gases, together with tiny amounts of ice, carbon and metals, swirled together to form a hot, dense mass which became the star known as the **Sun**.

Some of the solid material left over from the formation of the Sun collected into smaller globules. These became the **planets**.

When the newly formed Sun began to shine, it heated up the planets and the remains of the cloud. At the same time a thin stream of hot gas moved rapidly from the Sun's surface. This **solar wind** was less intense in the outer parts of the solar system, so it was very hot here...

...and very cold here.

After a few million years the solar wind died down and the heat became less intense. The surfaces of the planets became cooler. Chemical reactions between the substances in the planets gradually released gases. These gases formed the **atmospheres** of the planets.

Note: Surface gravity is the strength of the gravity force at the surface of the planet, relative to the Earth as 1.0.

Venus
Composition: Rocky
Distance from the Sun: 108 million kilometres
Orbital period: 224 days
Rotation period: 243 days
Surface gravity: 0.90
Number of moons: 0
Average surface temperature: 750 K

Mercury
Composition: Rocky
Distance from the Sun: 60 million kilometres
Orbital period: 88 days
Rotation period: 59 days
Surface gravity: 0.38
Number of moons: 0
Average surface temperature: 340 K

Jupiter
Composition: Mainly ice
Distance from the Sun: 778 million kilometres
Orbital period: 12 years
Rotation period: 10 hours
Surface gravity: 2.7
Number of moons: 16
Average surface temperature: 125 K

THINKING ABOUT: THE EARTH IN SPACE

Pluto ●
Composition: Ice and rock?
Distance from the Sun:
 5900 million kilometres
Orbital period: 248 years
Rotation period: 6 days
Surface gravity: 0›5?
Number of moons: 1
Average surface temperature: 40 K

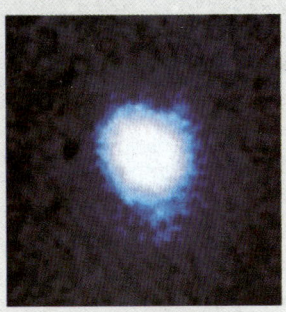

Earth ●
Composition: Rocky
Distance from the Sun:
 150 million kilometres
Orbital period: 365 days
Rotation period: 24 hours
Surface gravity: 1.0
Number of moons: 1
Average surface temperature: 289 K

Neptune ●
Composition: Ice and rock
Distance from the Sun:
 4497 million kilometres
Orbital period: 165 years
Rotation period: 22 hours
Surface gravity: 1.2
Number of moons: 7
Average surface temperature: 55 K

Mars ●
Composition: Rocky
Distance from the Sun:
 228 million kilometres
Orbital period: 2 years
Rotation period: 24 hours
Surface gravity: 0.38
Number of moons: 2
Average surface temperature: 200 K

Uranus ●
Composition: Ice and rock
Distance from the Sun:
 2870 million kilometres
Orbital period: 84 years
Rotation period: 23 hours
Surface gravity: 0.8
Number of moons: 14
Average surface temperature: 60 K

Saturn ●
Composition: Mainly ice
Distance from the Sun:
 1427 million kilometres
Orbital period: 12 years
Rotation period: 10 hours
Surface gravity: 1.2
Number of moons: 17
Average surface temperature: 163 K

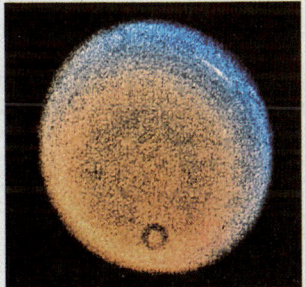

2. How can we travel in space?

When a large rocket blasts off, a huge force is needed to lift it from the launch pad.

But once the spacecraft is in space, no force is needed to keep it moving. Occasional small bursts from its rockets may be used to change its speed or direction.

To take off, the rocket engines must exert a large force to accelerate the rocket upwards. Starting from rest (speed = 0) the rocket has to reach a speed of 11 km/s. If the speed is less than 11 km/s, the rocket will eventually fall back to Earth. Rocket scientists can work out the size of engine force they need using Newton's second law of motion: $F = ma$.

$F = ma$
Net force = mass × acceleration
(Engine thrust − weight of rocket) = mass × acceleration

Notice that the net force on the rocket is the engine thrust (upwards) minus the weight of the rocket (the downwards force of gravity on the rocket itself).

Once the space vehicle is in deep space, far from the Earth, its rocket motors can be shut down. The spacecraft keeps on travelling in a straight line at the speed it had at the moment the motors were turned off.

This is an example of Newton's first law of motion: an object stays at rest or continues to move at steady speed in a straight line unless a force acts on it.

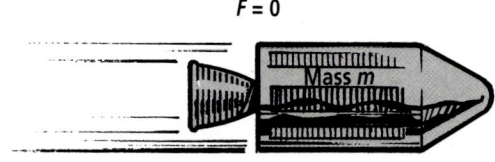

Steady speed v in a straight line

The Space Shuttle in the photo on the left has its engine shut down but it is *not* travelling in a straight line – it is **orbiting** the Earth, moving in a circular path high above the Earth's surface. The rocket motors do not need to exert any force to keep the spacecraft moving around its orbit at steady speed. *Thinking About 4* looks at circular motion and orbits in more detail.

Moving in space

If you are stationary and want to move, or if you are moving and want to speed up, you have to push back on something.

When the engine turns the wheel, the tyres of this trials bike push back on the ground. The ground exerts a forward push on the bike.

The propellor of a boat pushes water backwards as it spins. The water exerts a forward push on the boat.

These are all examples of Newton's third law of motion. Newton noticed that forces always occur in pairs: if object A exerts a force on object B, then object B exerts an equal force on object A, but in the opposite direction.

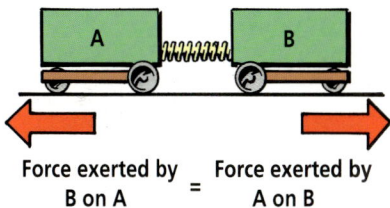

But this poses a problem for space travel – space is empty so there is nothing to push against. A rocket uses its own fuel as something to push against. In a rocket motor, fuel is burnt and pushed out of the back of the rocket at high speed. The backwards push of the rocket on the exhaust gases causes an equal and opposite push – the exhaust gases push the rocket forwards.

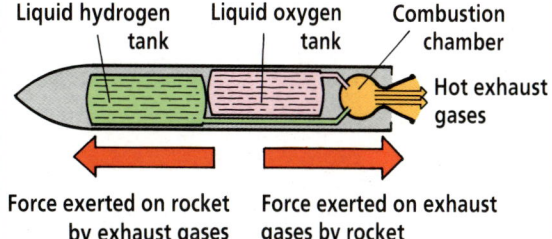

Because of this, a rocket must carry a very large amount of fuel at take-off. Notice the large extra fuel tanks on the Space Shuttle when launched (see photo on opposite page).

Taking it further: Rocket motion and momentum
The motion of a spacecraft illustrates the general law that **momentum is always conserved when objects interact**. Momentum is defined as mass × velocity.

Imagine a spacecraft at rest in deep space. Its momentum is zero, because its velocity is zero. The craft fires its motors. Some burnt fuel is pushed out of the back of the rocket motor. These moving gases have momentum in the backward direction. The spacecraft moves forward in reaction to the backward movement of the gases. The momentum of the spacecraft is equal to the momentum of the gases, but in the opposite direction. The *total* momentum of the spacecraft and gases is still zero.

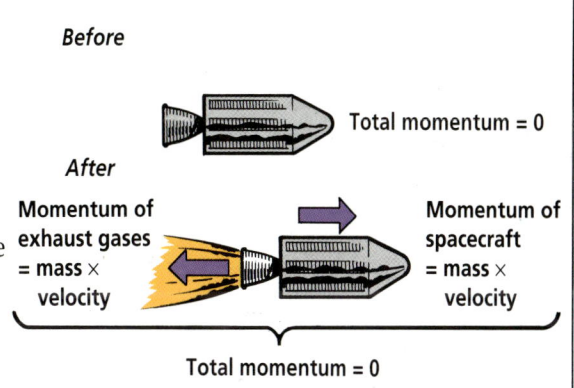

The total momentum is zero before and after the engine burn, but the spacecraft has started moving.

3. What happens when a spacecraft lifts off?

The first stage of a space flight is lift-off. Seeing what happens to the motion of objects which are fired or thrown upwards will help us (in *Thinking About 4*) to understand how spacecraft can stay in orbit round the Earth.

This is a strobe photo of a ball thrown upwards. The photo was taken in a dark room with a regularly flashing light. The camera shutter was kept open. The film shows the position of the ball every time there was a flash of light.

The time between the positions of the ball is always the same. Where the positions of the ball are close together, it was moving slowly – it did not move far between flashes. Where they are further apart, the ball was moving faster. You can see that the ball slowed down as it rose. The force of gravity pulling downwards on the ball made it slow down and eventually stop at the top of its flight.

This second strobe photo shows what happens if we watch the motion for a little longer. The force of gravity on the ball makes it accelerate as it falls back down.

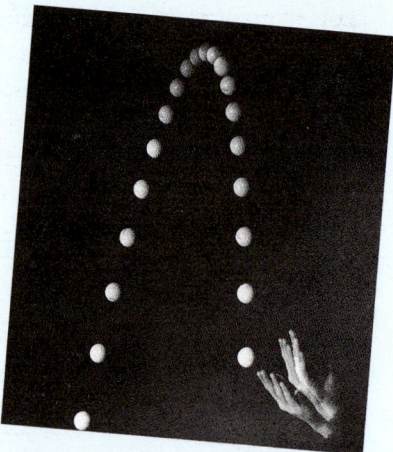

There is an upward force on the ball only at the moment when you throw it. Once it has left your hand, the only force acting on it is gravity – which is always downwards. A rocket *continues* to fire its motors as it lifts off. So there is a *continuous* upward thrust as it lifts off and ascends.

4. How are spacecraft able to stay in orbit round the Earth?

Some people think that a spacecraft can orbit the Earth, instead of falling back to the surface, because it has escaped from the Earth's gravity. But this is not correct. The pull of the Earth's gravity does get slightly less as the rocket gets higher, but it does not become zero.

One way to understand orbits is to think first about projectiles. A **projectile** is any object which is thrown forwards so that it has a horizontal velocity and is also acted upon by gravity.

Look carefully at this strobe photo of a projectile, and measure the distances on it with a ruler. You will find that the horizontal distance between the positions of the ball is always the same. The

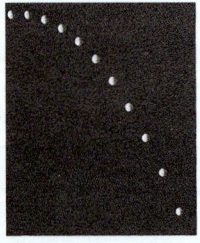

projectile has a steady horizontal speed. The distance between the vertical positions increases steadily as it falls. The projectile has a vertical acceleration – the acceleration due to gravity.

What would happen if you threw several projectiles horizontally from a high tower, at different speeds? Compact solid objects all fall vertically with the same acceleration, so all the projectiles would take the same time to reach the ground. But the distance they travel before landing depends on how fast they were thrown forwards – the greater the horizontal speed, the further the projectile will go.

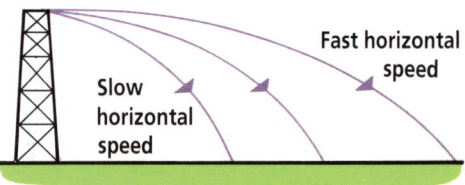

Isaac Newton worked on the motion of projectiles, and this idea led him to a 'thought experiment' – an experiment which he couldn't try out but which he could think through. He imagined a projectile fired horizontally from a high tower. The faster it was fired, the further it would go. But if he took into account the fact that the Earth is round, not flat, the projectile would travel further still.

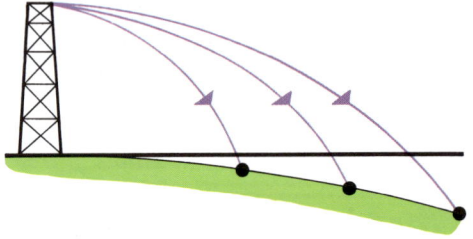

Newton realized that there must be a speed at which the falling of the projectile would be exactly matched by the curvature of the Earth's surface. If he could fire a projectile at this speed, it would go right round the Earth in a curved path. It would become a satellite in orbit.

THINKING ABOUT: THE EARTH IN SPACE

So satellites stay in orbit not because they have escaped from Earth's gravity, but *because* of Earth's gravity. The satellite is like a projectile. It is falling towards the Earth, but at exactly the same rate as the Earth's surface is curving away below it.

Anybody inside a falling container feels and appears weightless, so astronauts in an orbiting spacecraft experience the sensation of weightlessness.

5. What keeps things moving in a circle?

A satellite in Earth orbit is an example of circular motion. Circular motion always needs a force pulling towards the centre of the circle.

You can see this if you think of whirling a block tied to a string round above your head.

The tension force in the string keeps the block moving in a circle. If the string breaks, the block will fly off in a straight line in the direction it was travelling when the string broke.

The force towards the centre which keeps a satellite in orbit is the gravitational force of the Earth on the satellite. Although we tend to think of gravity as a force exerted by the Earth on other objects, in fact all objects exert a gravitational force on each other. The size of the force depends on the masses of the objects involved. The greater the masses, the bigger the gravitational force they exert on each other.

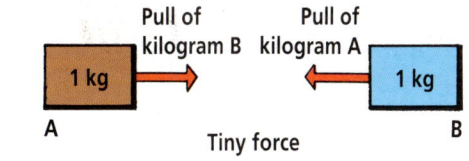

Both objects exert an equal force on each other.

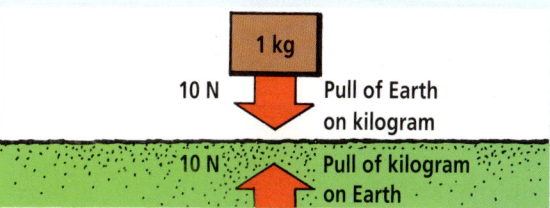

In this case, the kilogram pulls the Earth just as much as the Earth pulls the kilogram! This is another example of Newton's third law of motion: forces come in equal pairs.

The gravitational pull of any object decreases with distance. So the strength of the Earth's gravity gets less as you go further away from the Earth. But it never becomes completely zero.

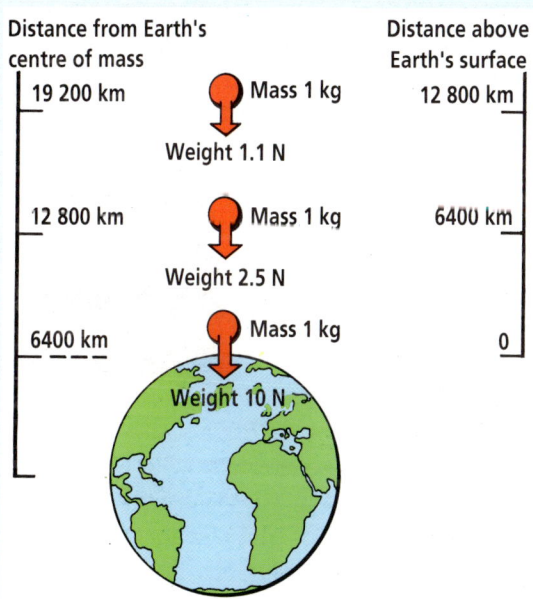

6. Weight and mass: what's the difference?

Changing weight

The **weight** of an object is the size of the gravity force which the Earth exerts on the object. This depends on the mass of the object and the gravity field at the place where you are weighing the object.

The gravitational force exerted by the Earth on a 1 kilogram mass is approximately 10 newtons. Another way to state this is to say that the strength of the Earth's gravitational field is 10 N/kg.

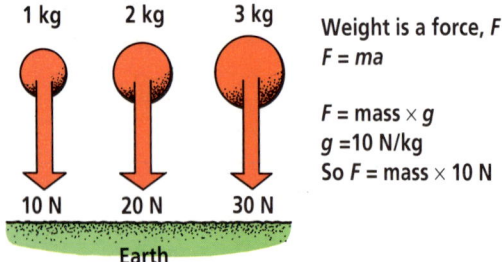

10 N/kg is the value of the gravitational field at the Earth's surface. If a kilogram mass were taken up in spacecraft to a height of 6400 km above the Earth's surface, its weight would be only 2.5 N (see the diagram on page 13). Doubling the distance from the centre of the Earth has reduced the gravity force by one-quarter. At this height, the strength of the Earth's gravitational field is just 2.5 N/kg. The gravitational field strength on the surface of the Moon is about 1.6 N/kg. So a kilogram mass on the Moon would weigh just 1.6 N.

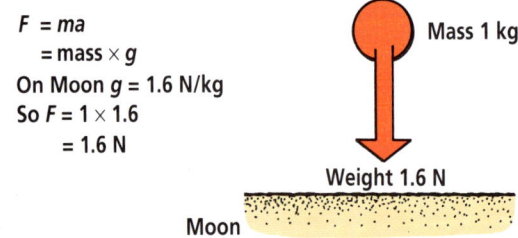

So the weight of an object depends on where the object is. If it stays on the Earth's surface, its weight only changes very slightly. (It is less if you go up a high mountain, but the difference is too small to detect easily.) If it is taken into space, its weight will change measurably. But its **mass** does not change.

Constant mass

An object's **mass** is always the same, no matter where it is. A one-kilogram mass is still a one-kilogram mass on the Moon.

The mass of a block of iron depends on how much iron is in the block, and does not change unless you remove or add some iron. But this doesn't explain very much. The scientific way of looking at mass is as a measure of how difficult it is to change the motion of an object. The force needed to accelerate an object is equal to its mass multiplied by the acceleration ($F = ma$). A large mass is hard to accelerate; it takes a large force. A smaller mass is more easily accelerated.

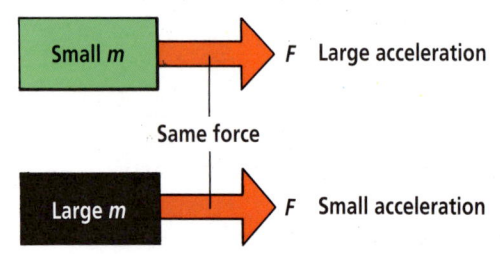

The mass of an object is always the same, so it always takes exactly the same force to give a kilogram mass a certain acceleration. With a given force the acceleration of the same mass will be the same on the Earth, in space far from Earth, on the Moon, or wherever.

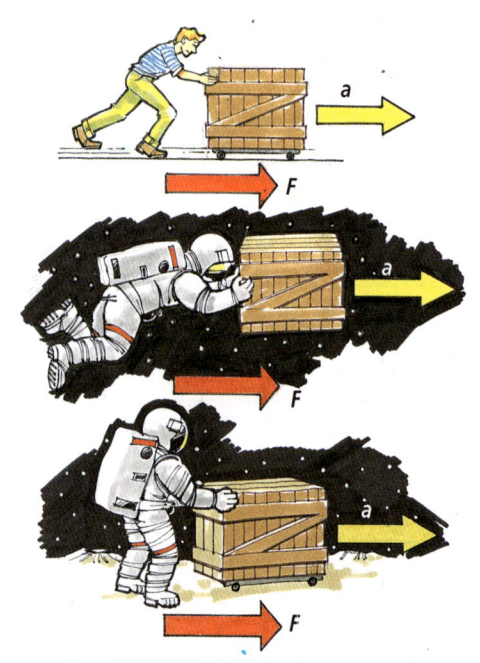

THINKING ABOUT: THE EARTH IN SPACE

7. How do we know about the Universe?

Our ideas about the Universe have come from using observation and theory in many different ways. Here are just a few examples.

The solar system

Often in the evening sky, you can see a very bright 'star'. It is not a star at all, but the planet Venus. How do we know it is not a star?

The early Greek and Persian astronomers, over 4000 years ago, noticed that some heavenly bodies move in a different way from most stars across the sky. Most stars move steadily across the night sky from east to west, just as the Sun does during the day. The whole pattern of stars moves together. But a few 'stars' slowly change their position against this fixed background. They were given the name 'planets', from a word meaning 'wanderer' in Greek. At this time astronomers thought that the Earth stayed still and the stars moved around it.

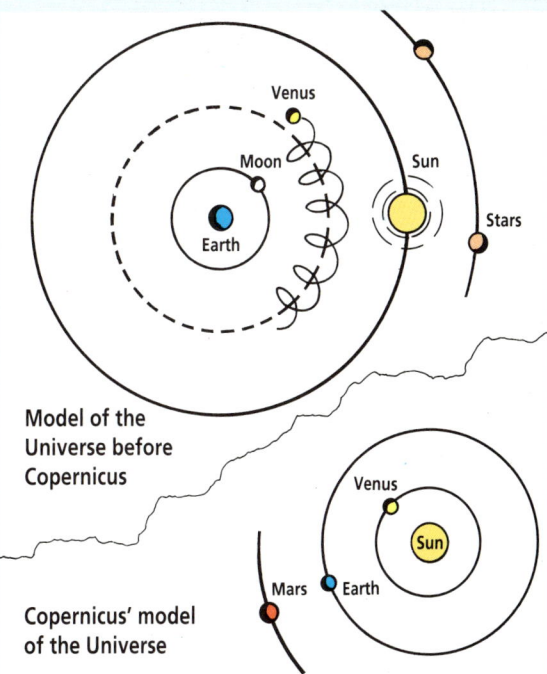

Model of the Universe before Copernicus

Copernicus' model of the Universe

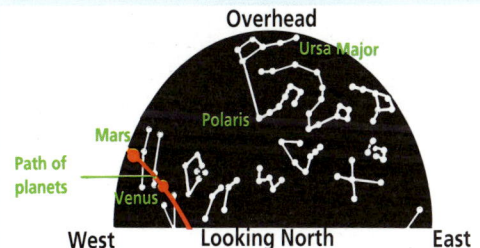

Stars appear to rotate slowly about the Pole Star (Polaris), while the planets move in a different way.

Astronomers plotted the path of the planets carefully and could predict their paths exactly. They had complicated ways of explaining this 'wandering' motion. In 1543, a Polish monk, Nikolaus Koppernigk (or Copernicus), wrote a book which said that the movement would be more simply explained if you thought of the Sun, and not the Earth, as the centre of the Universe. He said that the stars were very far away from the Earth. It was the spinning of the Earth on its axis that made the Sun and the stars look as if they were moving around the Earth. He suggested that the planets also move around the Sun, some closer to it than the Earth, others farther away. As the Earth moved round its orbit, it passed the other planets in their orbits. This was why the planets appeared to move against the background of stars.

The observations of the ancient astronomers had led to a theory about the Universe and how the different bodies move. Now Copernicus had shown how the same observations could be explained by a simpler and more elegant theory. Using new and better observations of the exact positions of the planets, Johannes Kepler in 1609 was able to show that the paths of the planets were ellipses, not perfect circles. But he could not provide any explanation for this shape of orbit. The final piece of the jigsaw was supplied by Newton's theory of universal gravity (all masses attract all other masses with a gravitational force, *Thinking About 5*, page 13). Newton showed how a force of attraction between the Sun and a planet would result in an orbit of exactly the shape Kepler had shown.

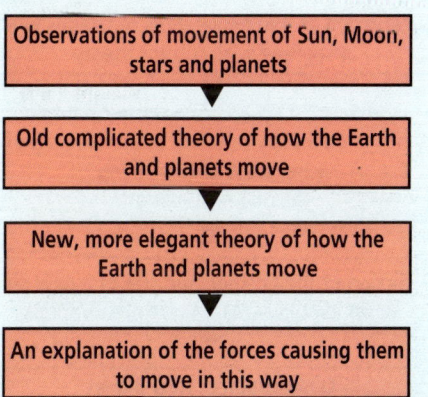

The discovery of Neptune

If there was only one planet moving around the Sun, it would move in a perfect ellipse. But there are several planets, and each planet exerts a gravitational force on all the other planets. This is much smaller than the gravitational force of the Sun on the planets, but it is enough to cause small 'wobbles' in the orbits, making them less than perfect ellipses.

In the early 1800s, six planets (in addition to the Earth) were known: Mercury, Venus, Mars, Jupiter, Saturn and Uranus. The first five can be seen with the naked eye; Uranus had been discovered by William Herschel using a telescope in 1781. Detailed observations of the orbit of Uranus, however, showed that it had more 'wobbles' than could be explained by the gravitational attractions of the other known planets. Was Newton's theory of gravitation wrong?

Scientists did not reject Newton's theory. Instead they looked for another explanation. Perhaps there was another planet having an effect on Uranus, that was further from the Sun than Uranus. Quite independently, two astronomers, John Adams in England (1845) and Urbain le Verrier in France (1846), used the wobbles in Uranus's orbit to make the same prediction about where the undiscovered planet should be. No one took Adams seriously because he was a young student. But they did look where le Verrier suggested – and they found the planet Neptune.

```
Explanation of how the planets move,
based on Newton's laws of motion and his law of
gravitation
            ↓
Observation of odd movements of Uranus which
disagreed with current theory
            ↓
Theory not immediately rejected; astronomers looked for
other ways of explaining
the odd observations
            ↓
Prediction of the position and size of a new planet
which would explain these observations
            ↓
Observation of new planet
```

Pulsars

In the summer of 1964, Jocelyn Bell was a research student at the radio astronomy observatory in Cambridge. She had helped other students to build a radio telescope and was now using it to study how radio waves from distant galaxies are affected by the 'solar wind' (a thin, hot gas that streams out from the Sun). The radio signals picked up by the telescope were recorded by a pen which made a wavy line on a moving strip of paper. Bell was analysing the records when she noticed an unusual 'blip'. There was one on the chart from the day before, at just about the same time.

Jocelyn Bell

Anthony Hewish

Her supervisor, Anthony Hewish, agreed that the 'blip' was odd and they both began to check it out. It was a series of regular pulses with $1\frac{1}{3}$ seconds between them. It seemed as though it must be due to some equipment or other artificial source. But a detailed check showed that it appeared at intervals of exactly 23 hours and 56 minutes – not a whole day, but at the time when exactly the same stars were overhead. (The difference of four minutes is due to the Earth's motion round the Sun; it takes just a little less than 24 hours for the Earth to point in the same direction again in space.) This suggested strongly that the pulsing signal came from space.

Another radio telescope checked the observation and found the same pulses. Meanwhile Bell and Hewish found two more pulsing sources in other parts of the sky. No one could explain what caused the pulses but it seemed that they might come from some sort of star. A journalist gave these new sources the name **pulsars**.

Astronomers then tried to find explanations for the pulses. The current theory is that pulsars are collapsed stars made almost entirely of neutrons. As they collapse, they spin faster and faster. They emit a beam of radio waves in one direction (the reason for this is not known). So they behave like a lighthouse and an observer on Earth sees a pulsing (or flashing) beam.

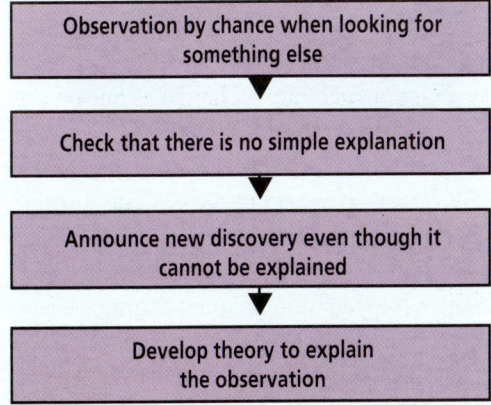

Black holes

If the discovery of pulsars is an example of observation coming before theory, then the discovery of black holes is the opposite. Astronomers had long believed that stars go through a life cycle which depends on their size. Some types of stars, called white dwarfs, collapse when their fuel is used up (page 85 gives more information about nuclear fusion reactions which fuel stars). The reason for the collapse is the gravitational attraction between the particles of material that makes up the star. The star becomes a super-dense **neutron star**, only a few kilometres across but with a greater mass than the Sun.

As the star's matter packs closer and closer together, the gravitational attraction increases (the size of the gravitational force between two masses depends on their distance apart, see *Thinking About 5*). The neutron star may collapse further until its gravitational field is so strong that even light, travelling at 300 000 km/s, cannot escape from it. No light can escape, so the star has become a **black hole**.

You may think that black holes are a new idea. The term 'black hole' *is* quite new, but the idea that such things might exist was first suggested by a Cambridge astronomer, John Michell, in 1783.

Since then the basic theory which leads to the prediction of black holes has been quite widely accepted. So people began to think of ways of observing a black hole. That might seem like an impossible task – how can you observe something which doesn't emit any light?

Many stars occur in pairs, rotating around each other. If one star in a pair was a black hole, then the other would seem to be rotating around nothing. And some stars like this *have* been seen. It may be, of course, that the other star in the pair is just too dim to be seen, but other observations convince some astronomers that a few of these pairs consist of a visible star and a black hole.

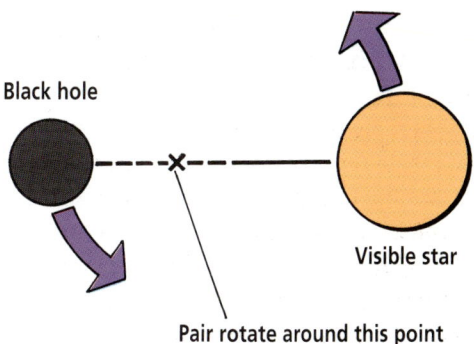

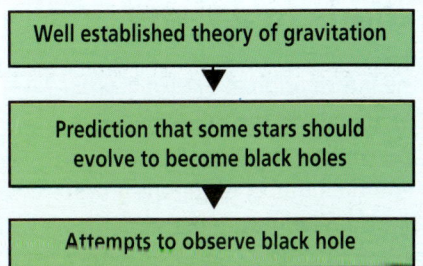

The method of science?

It would be hard to argue that these four astronomical discoveries have been made by following the same method of science. Sometimes observations are made by chance. On other occasions a theoretical prediction comes first. Observation always plays a part, and so does theory (or explanation). The history of our knowledge of the Universe shows some of the unpredictable ways in which observation and theory depend on each other to build a science.

Things to do

The Earth in Space

Things to try out

1 You can make a rocket-propelled vehicle by attaching a Sparklets capsule firmly to a trolley and then breaking the seal on the capsule. Take care – it can go quite fast! Design an investigation to measure the size of the force exerted by the Sparklets bulb rocket.

Points to discuss

2 Space exploration is expensive. It is estimated that it cost the USA 25 billion dollars to put a person on the Moon. Discuss with others in your class whether you think it is right to spend these large sums on space exploration. Make a list of the advantages of exploring space, and another list of other uses the money spent on space exploration might be put to.

Questions to answer

3 Use the information in *Thinking About 1* on pages 8-9 to answer the following:
(a) Is there a link between the surface gravity of a planet and the number of moons it has?
(b) Is there a relationship between the composition of a planet and its distance from the Sun?
(c) Explain in your own words the meaning of the terms 'orbital period' and 'rotational period'. Is there any relationship between the orbital and rotational periods of a planet?
(d) Make a bar graph showing the average surface temperatures of the planets in the solar system. Put the bars in order of increasing distance of the planets from the Sun. Write a brief explanation of the pattern you observe in these figures.

4 An astronaut goes on a space walk outside his spacecraft. He uses a Manned Manoeuvring Unit (MMU) to move himself around. This has four small rockets pointing in directions U, D, L and R.

(a) The astronaut fires rocket R for 5 seconds. Describe carefully what happens to him during this 5-second period and for the next 5 seconds afterwards.
(b) Sketch a speed–time graph to summarize your answer to **(a)**.
(c) The astronaut wants to move across to repair a solar panel which is upwards and to the right of his present position. Explain which rockets he should fire to get to the solar panel and to stop once he is there.
(d) Whilst on his spacewalk, rocket D jams at half throttle. What will happen if the astronaut does nothing about this? What would you advise him to do to correct it?

5 A tennis ball takes exactly 3 seconds to fall from the top of a tall building to the ground. If the ball is now thrown horizontally with a speed of 20 m/s from the top of the same building, how far from the bottom of the building will it land?

6 Forces always come in pairs. In each of these situations, say what the other force in the pair is. Copy the diagram and mark both forces clearly on it.

Introducing EVOLUTION

EVOLUTION 19

Retriever

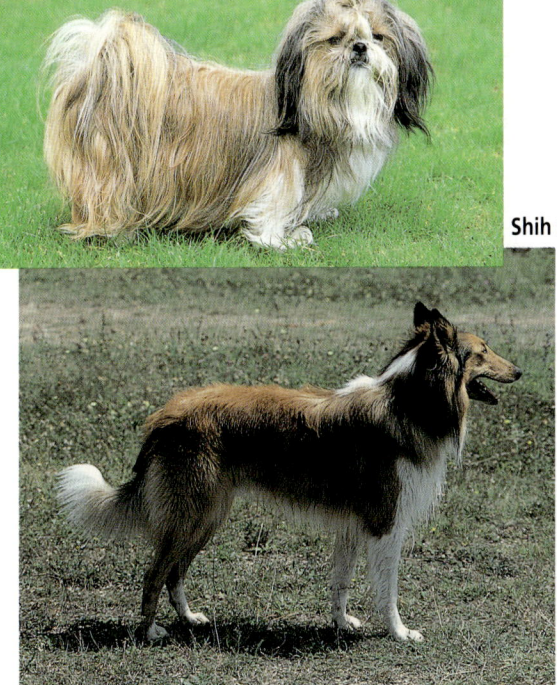

Shih tzu

Bloodhound

Collie

Husky

In nature, any species is made up of many individuals which have different characteristics.

Some individuals have characteristics which are better suited to their environment than others. They are more likely to survive, so they are more likely to breed and leave offspring, which may inherit these characteristics. The **survival of the fittest** individuals means that a species can gradually change in response to environmental change. This change is called **evolution**.

Dog breeders speed up this change by **selective breeding**. They select individuals to breed together in order to produce offspring with particular characteristics.

Look at the pictures.
1. What features do the dogs have in common?
2. What features are unique to each breed?
3. The dogs have been bred for different purposes. What do you think these are?
4. How do the features of each dog make it suitable for its purpose?

IN THIS CHAPTER YOU WILL FIND OUT
- about Charles Darwin and the theory of evolution
- how characteristics are inherited
- about genes and chromosomes
- about DNA
- about genetic engineering.

Looking at

The work of Darwin and Wallace

The theory of evolution

The stamps opposite were issued in 1982 to commemorate the death of Charles Darwin. He is best remembered for the theory of evolution by natural selection. But he was not the only person to propose the theory. On 1 July 1858 a paper by Charles Darwin and Alfred Russel Wallace was read to a meeting of members of the Linnean Society at Burlington House in London. The paper was entitled 'On the tendency of species to form varieties; and on the perpetuation of varieties and species by natural means of selection'. The theory of evolution was announced!

> 1 *Thinking About 1* on page 28 explains how new varieties can form from existing organisms by natural selection. This was the basis of Darwin and Wallace's paper. Find out where people believed all the different organisms came from, before there was any talk of evolution.

The development of Darwin's theory

Charles Darwin was a careful observer and collector of evidence. In 1831–7 he worked as a naturalist on board HMS *Beagle* which was exploring the Pacific Ocean and South America. This was when he started to form his ideas about evolution.

Darwin was very curious about how the unusual plants and animals had formed on the Galapagos Islands, off the coast of South America.

HMS *Beagle* in the Straits of Magellan

He was particularly interested in the finches there. Although they were related to each other, they represented several different species. Each species had a beak suited to its lifestyle. Some were ground finches and some were tree finches. All the ground finches had beaks suited to eating seeds. Most, but not all, the tree finches had beaks suited to eating insects.

Darwin wondered whether they had all come from one species of finch. Perhaps birds well adapted to eating particular foods had survived and bred, and natural selection had eventually resulted in several new species with different feeding characteristics.

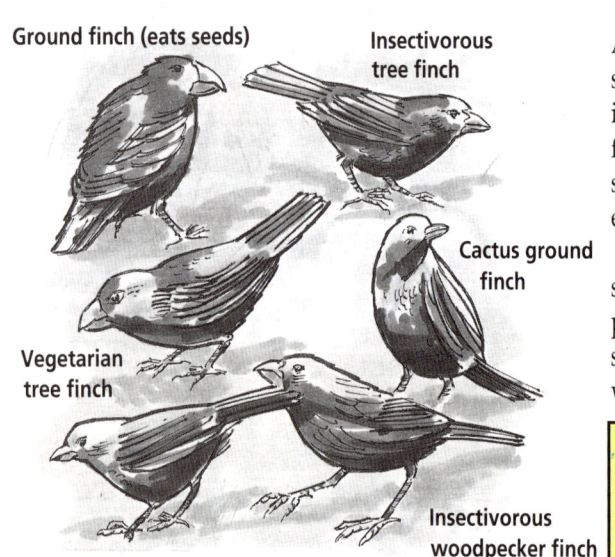

> 2 Look at the Galapagos finches shown here. Suggest how their beaks are adapted to suit their food sources.
> 3 What is the difference between a variety and a species? How might the different species of the Galapagos finches have evolved from one original species?

Putting it all together

In 1842 Darwin wrote a brief extract of his theory of evolution by natural selection. Over the following years he collected all the facts he could find on variation, cross-breeding experiments, fossils, classification and comparative anatomy. In 1856 he finally started to prepare a book in which his ideas could be fully presented and supported with evidence. His friends encouraged him to hurry to publication but he delayed to solve every problem he came across. By 1858 he had completed eleven chapters but had more to write.

On 18 June 1858 Darwin received a letter from Alfred Russel Wallace asking for an opinion on his essay entitled 'On the tendency of varieties to depart indefinitely from the original type'. It was clear that Wallace had independently arrived at similar conclusions on evolution.

Alfred Russel Wallace

Wallace was a naturalist who travelled all over the world. From 1854 to 1858 he toured Malaysia, recording the many different species he found there. In 1858 he caught malaria and, while recovering, had a sudden inspiration regarding how species might evolve by natural selection. Over the next two evenings he wrote his views in an essay. It was this essay that he sent to Darwin.

Both men had arrived at the same theory by different means – Darwin by painstaking collection of information followed by detailed analysis and testing, and Wallace in a flash of inspiration.

Presenting the theory

Darwin wished for Wallace's essay to be published in a scientific journal but his scientist friends persuaded him that in the interests of science a joint paper should be prepared. The result was the presentation to the Linnean Society.

There was never any rivalry between Darwin and Wallace. On receiving Wallace's essay, Darwin was prepared to give up any first claim to the theory of evolution by natural selection.

The Origin of Species

Darwin now worked at completing his book. In November 1859 *The Origin of Species* was published. It showed how the theory of natural selection could explain the diversity of living things, and how all living things, including humans, could have evolved from earlier organisms. It created great controversy and changed the course of human thought.

> 4 Look at your answer to question 1.
> Why do you think that *The Origin of Species* caused such great controversy?

The controversy went on for some time. This cartoon is from the *London Sketch Book*, May 1874, one of many reactions to *The Origin of Species*.

Looking at Fossils

22   *LOOKING AT: EVOLUTION*

Fossils are traces of organisms that lived millions of years ago. Most fossils are bits of animals or plants or the impressions of where something walked or fell into soft mud. It is very rare to find a fossil of a complete organism.

Individual fossils do not give us a great deal of information about evolution. But by comparing fossils of different ages we can infer how an organism has gradually changed over time.

Look at the drawings of the five different fossils on the question card. Compare each with the drawings on the reference card for that organism.

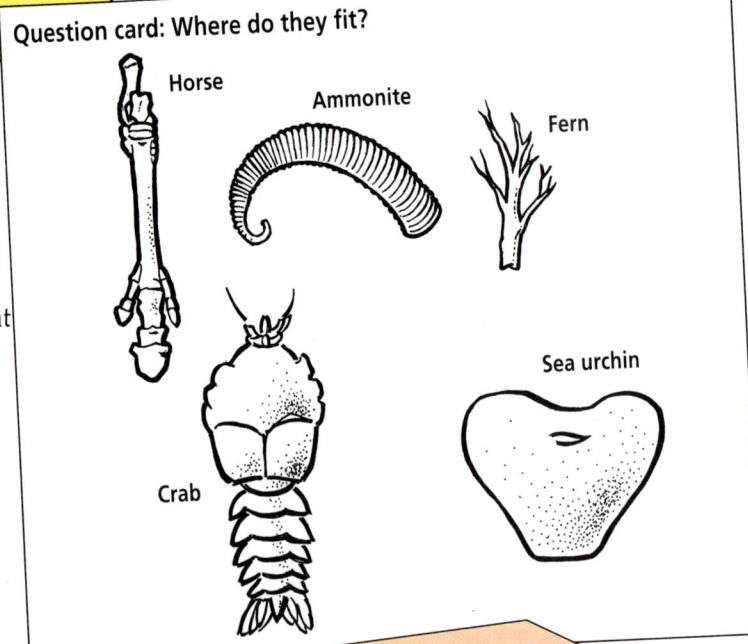

Question card: Where do they fit?
Horse, Ammonite, Fern, Crab, Sea urchin

1. Where do you think each fossil fits in the evolutionary sequence of development of the organism?
2. What features of each fossil did you use to reach a decision?
3. Now look at the geological time chart at the foot of the spread.
   Estimate the age of each of the fossils shown (a) on the question card and (b) on the reference cards.

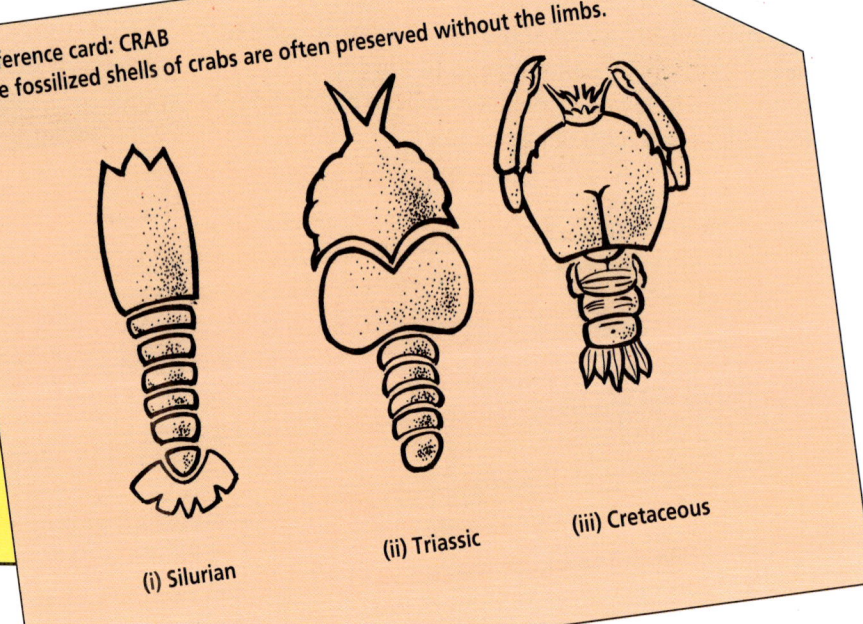

Reference card: CRAB
The fossilized shells of crabs are often preserved without the limbs.
(i) Silurian   (ii) Triassic   (iii) Cretaceous

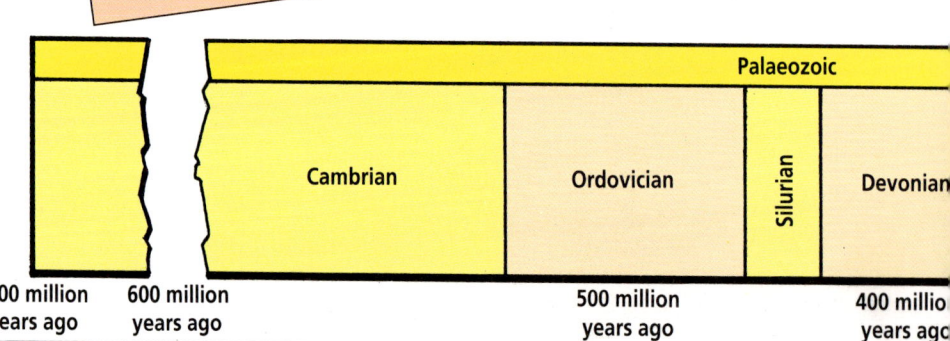

Palaeozoic | Cambrian | Ordovician | Silurian | Devonian

4500 million years ago   600 million years ago   500 million years ago   400 million years ago

LOOKING AT: EVOLUTION: 23

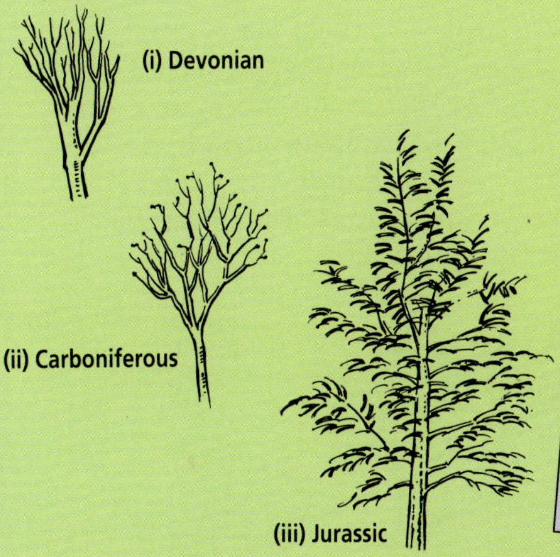

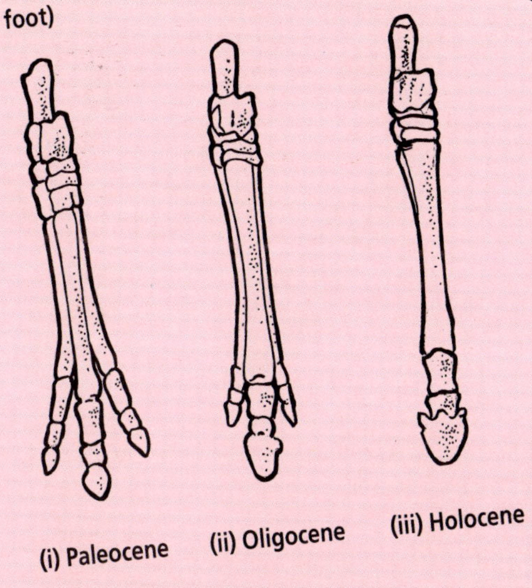

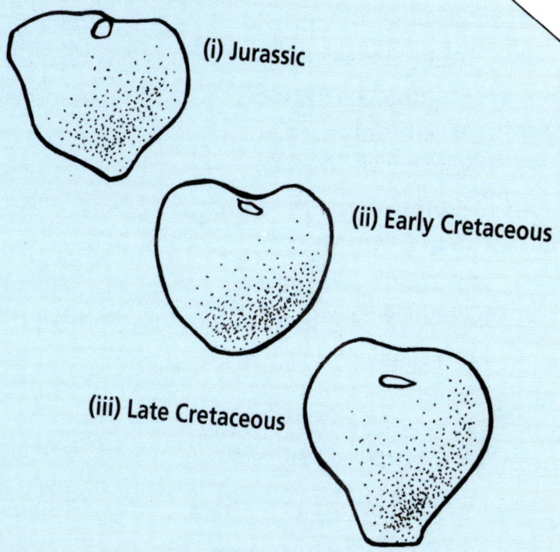

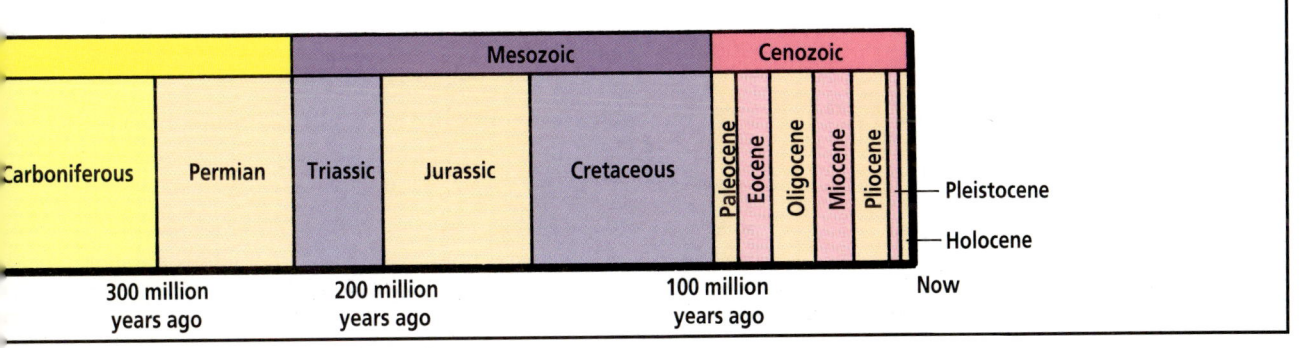

Looking at Peas in a Pod

LOOKING AT: EVOLUTION

If you buy peas in a greengrocer, it is likely that all the peas inside a pod will be similar. They will look the same and taste the same. This is because plant breeders have produced varieties of plants which always produce peas with an appearance and flavour which are popular. To do this they have to understand how the characteristics of appearance and flavour pass from one generation to another – how they are inherited.

Investigating patterns of inheritance

The first person to explain inheritance was an Austrian monk named Gregor Mendel. He joined the Augustinian monastery at Brunn in Austria (now Brno in Czechoslovakia) in 1842 when he was nineteen. He studied natural history and mathematics at the University of Vienna and returned to the monastery where he stayed until his death in 1884.

Mendel made a study of pea plants in the monastery garden. He noticed several paired characteristics, such as that pea plants grew either tall or short, that the pods could be either green or yellow, and that the peas could be round or wrinkled. He wondered what determined the characteristics of each pea plant.

Pea plants naturally self-pollinate. Mendel could prevent this by removing the stamens. He could then cross-pollinate plants by moving pollen from one plant to another using a fine brush.

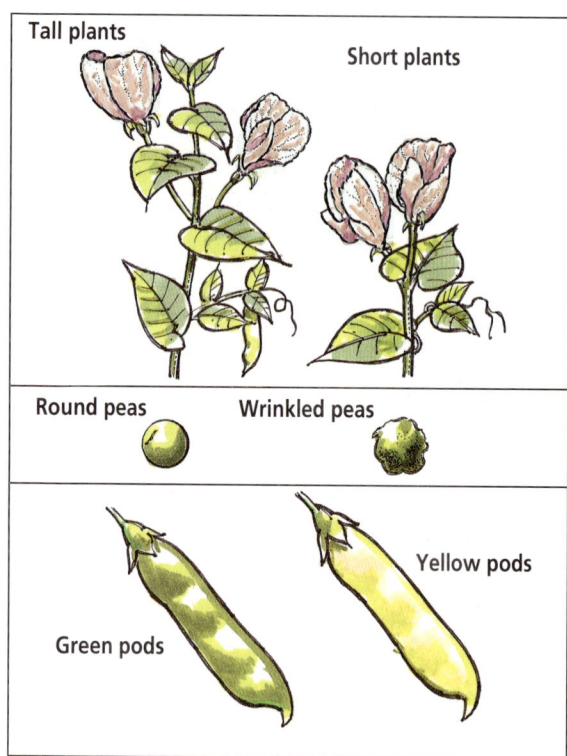

Some pea plant characteristics studied by Mendel

Stigma (female part – fertilization happens when pollen lands here)

Stamen (male part that produces pollen)

Mendel's experiments

Mendel cross-pollinated tall plants and short plants. He collected the peas and grew plants from them. Instead of the expected medium-sized plants, he grew only tall plants.

He let these tall plants self-pollinate and again grew plants from the peas that resulted. The result was surprising – some plants grew tall and others short. Mendel counted them and found there were three times as many tall plants as short plants.

1 The shape of the pea flower means that pea plants naturally self-pollinate. Pea plants tend to be pure-breeding – tall plants always produce more tall plants, short plants produce short plants, etc. Use *Thinking About 4* on page 30 to explain how these two facts are related.

2 If Mendel had cross-pollinated tall plants with short plants, collected 1000 peas and planted them, approximately how many tall plants and how many short plants would result?

Mendel repeated this experiment with other characteristics such as round and wrinkled peas and yellow and green pods. He had similar results.

Drawing conclusions

Here are the results from one of Mendel's experiments.

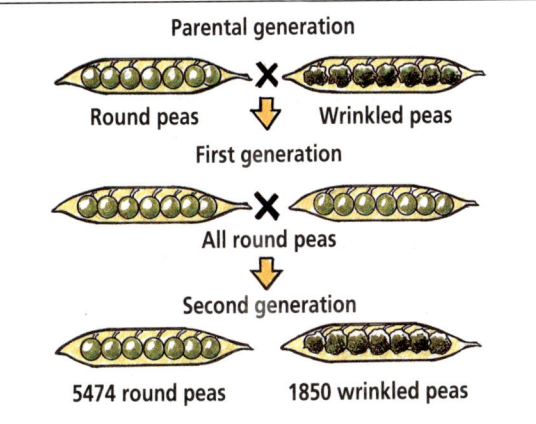

Mendel decided that the first generation of peas must have inherited some factor for wrinkled peas, even though all the peas were round. They then passed this factor on, which is why there were some wrinkled peas in the second generation.

He concluded that:
(a) The characteristics of a pea plant correspond to factors which are inherited.
(b) Characteristics occur in pairs, for example peas are either round or wrinkled. Each parent passes only one factor for each characteristic to the offspring.
(c) Some factors dominate others, so that first generation plants, which have factors for both round and wrinkled peas, have only round peas.

---

3 Which generation was cross-pollinated?
4 Which generation was self-pollinated?
5 What was the ratio of round peas to wrinkled peas in the second generation?
6 Look at *Thinking About 4* on page 30. Draw a table to explain the ratio of round peas to wrinkled peas in the second generation.

Gregor Mendel – a forgotten scientist

Mendel reported his studies in a paper written for the Brunn Society for the Study of Natural Science. Unfortunately nobody realized the significance of his work and it was largely forgotten for about 30 years, until rediscovered by other scientists carrying out similar experiments.

The secret of Mendel's success

Other scientists had tried to study inheritance before Mendel but, because they recorded large numbers of variations, they had difficulty explaining their observations. Mendel was successful because he was patient, asked precise questions and used logical methods of investigation. His mathematics training also helped.

(a) He chose to study pea plants which usually self-pollinated, but which were easy to cross-pollinate.
(b) He studied a small number of carefully chosen characteristics such as whether peas were round or wrinkled, or pods green or yellow.
(c) He used pure-bred plants that he had bred for two years prior to starting his experiments so he was sure that they would not show unexpected characteristics unrelated to his experiments.
(d) He used large numbers of plants to make certain that his results were not due to chance.
(e) He spent a long time over his experiments, following his cross-bred plants through several generations.

---

7 Mendel's work was not well publicized in his lifetime. If such discoveries were made today they would make headline news. Write a script for a radio news programme reporting the importance of Mendel's work.

In brief

Evolution

1 Individuals of a species show variation in their **characteristics**, such as hair colour or eye colour.

2 The characteristics of an individual are determined by the interaction of **inherited factors** and **environmental factors.**

Plants with the same genetic factors grow differently in different soils.

Plants with different genetic factors grow differently in the same soil.

3 Individuals with characteristics best suited to their environments are most likely to survive and reproduce. This is called **natural selection**. For example, a moth the same colour as its surroundings is less likely to be eaten than one with a contrasting colour. The offspring of the camouflaged moth are likely to be camouflaged as well. Over a period of time, the proportion of camouflaged moths increases. The characteristics of the population change. This change or **evolution** is due to the **survival of the fittest**.

4 The theory of evolution by natural selection explains how organisms can change over very long periods of time, and how present-day organisms could have developed from earlier forms.

5 Selective breeding is used to produce plants and animals with desirable characteristics. This is called **artificial selection**.

6 Fossils give evidence about the types of organisms that existed in the past.

7 There are conflicting theories on the origin of present-day lifeforms.

8 Cells contain thread-like structures called **chromosomes**. These carry coded information needed for the control and development of the organism.

9 All the cells of an individual come from one original cell. This is created when the male and female parent cells join. Each parent cell contributes half the final number of chromosomes to the new cell.

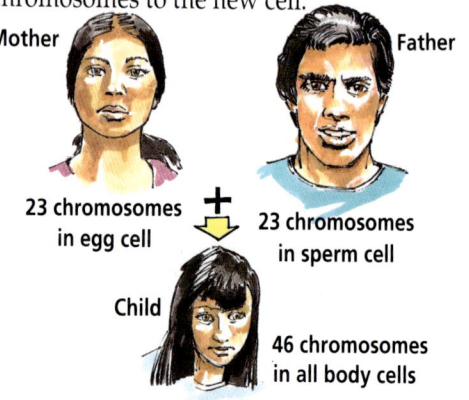

10 Chromosomes carry **genes**. A gene is responsible for the inheritance of a particular characteristic.

Different forms of a gene are called **alleles**. Different alleles cause different characteristics. For example, some people can roll their tongue and others cannot. These are two alternative characteristics. People who can roll their tongue have the tongue-rolling allele, those who cannot have the non-tongue-rolling allele. Both are alleles of the tongue-rolling gene.

11 Chromosomes occur in pairs. The chromosomes in these **homologous** pairs look the same as each other and carry the same genes. However, each chromosome may have a different allele for a particular gene.

Two homologous pairs of chromosomes

12 Within a pair of alleles, one is usually **dominant**. This means that if both alleles are present in an individual's chromosomes, the individual shows only the dominant characteristic. The allele for the hidden characteristic is called the **recessive** allele. For example, in peas, the tall allele is dominant over the short allele, which is recessive.

When neither allele is dominant, there is a mixing of characteristics. This is called **co-dominance**. In purebred Longhorn cattle, crossbreeding a white cow with a red bull results in roan calves with a mixture of red and white hairs (see photo on page 34).

13 It is possible to identify patterns in the way certain characteristics are inherited. From these patterns we can predict the chances of a characteristic being inherited in the offspring of certain parents.

14 Whether you are male or female is determined by the genes on your **sex chromosomes**. Females have two X chromosomes. Males have one X and one Y chromosome.

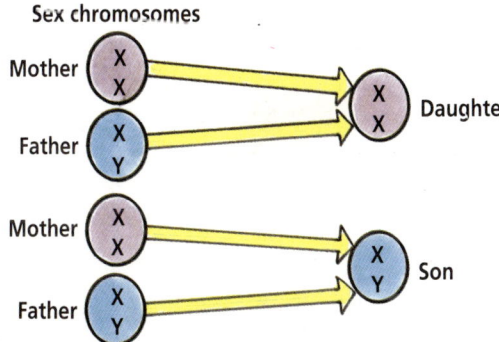

15 Characteristics controlled by genes, such as fur colour, are **inherited**. **Acquired** characteristics, such as large muscles resulting from bodybuilding, are not inherited.

16 Chromosomes contain the chemical **DNA**. A molecule of DNA consists of two long chains. These chains are twisted together to form a shape called a **double helix**.

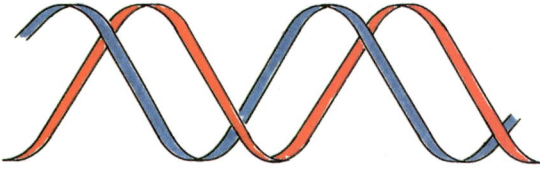

Part of a DNA molecule

17 Genes are particular segments of the DNA chain. The positions of particular genes can be mapped along the length of a chromosome.

18 The DNA chain can be changed in such a way that genes on it change. These changes are called **mutations**. Mutations can result in changed characteristics. For example, a mutation which produces an extra chromosome in humans causes Down's syndrome.

19 Mutations are natural events. Not all mutations are harmful. Some chemicals and other environmental factors such as radiation increase the rate of mutation.

20 There are techniques which can deliberately alter an organism's DNA and so change its characteristics. These are called **genetic engineering**.

21 Large numbers of genetically identical individuals can be raised from a single parent. This is called **gene cloning**.

22 Genetic engineering and gene cloning have resulted in benefits for humans. However, great care has to be taken to ensure that genetically engineered organisms are not accidentally released into the natural environment.

Diabetic people have to inject themselves with the hormone insulin. Before genetically engineered human insulin was available, insulin from pigs and cattle was used.

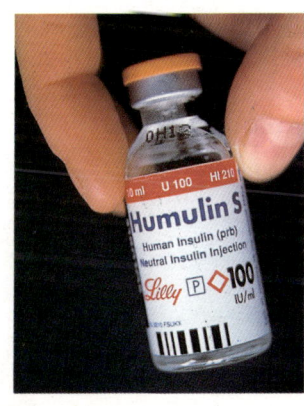

Thinking about Evolution

1. What is natural selection?

Variation

The characteristics of an individual are determined by the interaction of inherited **genes** and **environmental factors**. Individuals within a population of a species show **variation** in their characteristics. This variation increases the chances of survival of the genes carried by the species. The photo shows variation in corn (maize) cobs:

What happens if the environment changes?

Individuals with the characteristics best suited to the new environment are most likely to survive and reproduce. They produce offspring with similar inherited characteristics to themselves. Over long periods of time there is an increase in the proportion of individuals that are well adapted. The species characteristics change in response to a changing environment – the species **evolves**. Characteristics that are not well adapted gradually die out.

So the individuals best adapted to the environment are selected – this is called **natural selection**. It results in the **survival of the fittest**.

A group of well-adapted individuals (a **variety**) may breed together and evolve until they can no longer breed with other members of the species. A new species has evolved. In this way natural selection can explain how present-day organisms could have evolved over millions of years from earlier life forms.

Whole species such as the dodo can die out or become extinct if they do not evolve quickly enough in a changing environment.

Evolution – fact or theory?

The theory of evolution by natural selection cannot be fully tested, but it is supported by a large number of observations for which we cannot find a better explanation. However, some people are not convinced by this and reject the theory.

2. What is artificial selection?

We can breed organisms with particular desirable characteristics. By selecting individuals with the required characteristics and allowing them to reproduce we can produce more individuals with similar characteristics. For example, we can develop crop plants with a capacity for high yield or good resistance to pests, or breed cattle which give a high milk yield or good meat.

Beef cattle and dairy cows are the results of artificial selection.

3. Why are chromosomes important?

Inside the nucleus of every cell is a set of thread-like structures called **chromosomes**. These carry **genes** which determine the inherited characteristics of the individual. Genes are passed on from generation to generation.

Each cell in your body has 46 chromosomes in its nucleus (except for the sex cells which have 23). A fruit fly's body cells have 8 chromosomes and a pea plant's have 14.

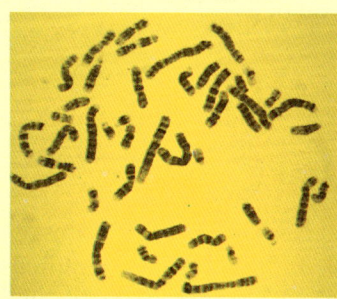

Human chromosomes magnified 1500 times.

THINKING ABOUT: EVOLUTION

Chromosomes and sexual reproduction

All your body cells came originally from one single cell – the fertilized egg.

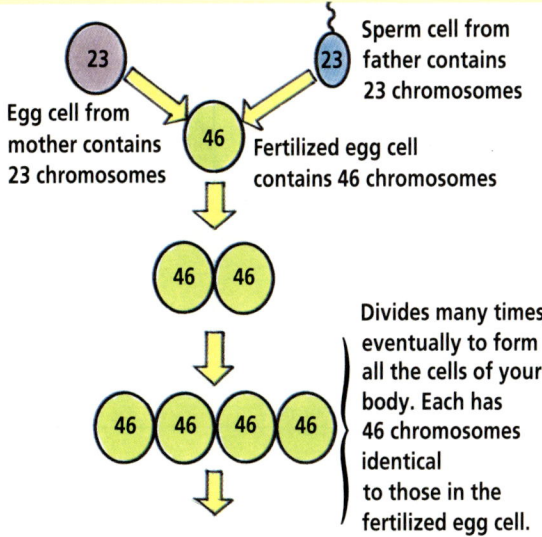

How cells divide

Chromosomes have a special ability to replicate themselves when a cell divides, so that the two new cells each have a set of chromosomes exactly the same as the old cell. As chromosomes carry genes, this means the new cells are genetically identical to the old one.

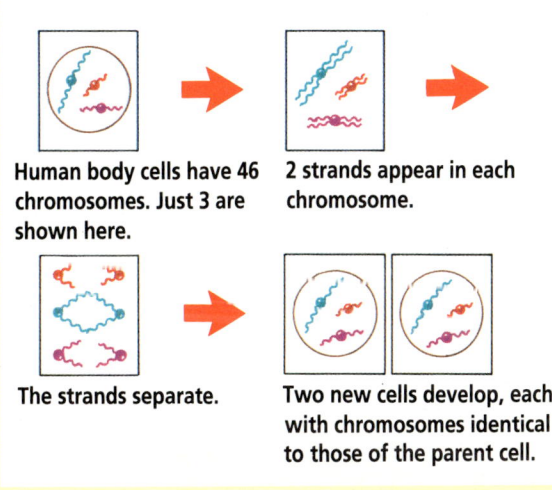

Homologous pairs of chromosomes

Chromosomes are present in cells as **homologous pairs**. The members of a homologous pair look identical and carry the same set of genes as each other. One member of each homologous pair came originally from the mother and one from the father.

Genes and alleles

Genes can have different forms. These different forms are called **alleles** and are usually present in pairs. For example, one allele of a particular hair colour gene is black and another is red. (There are several hair colour genes – others may give blond or mousy hair.)

Each homologous chromosome may carry different alleles of a gene. The allele on the chromosome that originated from the mother may be black and that on the chromosome from the father may be red. Or the maternal allele may be red and the paternal one black. Alternatively, both chromosomes may carry the red allele or both may carry the black allele.

An individual with two red alleles will have red hair. An individual with two black alleles will have black hair. An individual with one red and one black allele will have black hair too. This is because the black hair allele is **dominant** over the red hair allele. The red hair allele only shows up when present on both homologous chromosomes. It is hidden when there is a black hair allele present. It is **recessive**.

This girl has two red hair alleles.

This boy may have two black hair alleles, or he may have one red and one black. You cannot tell by looking at him.

4. How can we predict patterns of inheritance?

You cannot say for certain what characteristics will be inherited from a given pair of parents. But you can calculate the *chances* of various characteristics being shown by the offspring.

For example, in guinea pigs the gene for coat colour has two alleles, one for black and one for brown. The black allele is dominant over the brown allele. Let **B** represent the black allele and **b** the brown allele.

If a group of black guinea pigs have been mated with only black guinea pigs over many generations, eventually a pure strain will result in which all offspring will be black. A pure strain of black guinea pigs will have alleles **BB** and a pure strain of brown guinea pigs **bb**.

If a pure-bred black guinea pig and a pure-bred brown guinea pig are mated, you can calculate the probability of the coat colours in a litter like this:

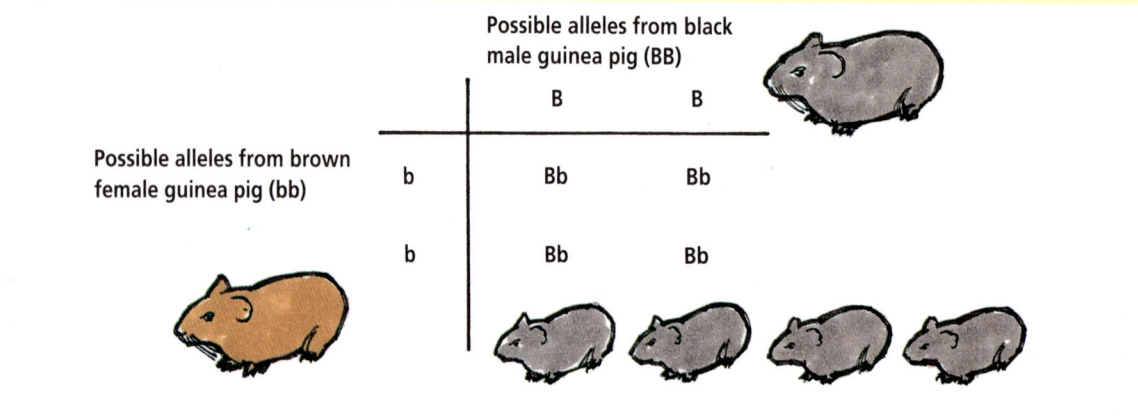

Thus all the litter will have alleles **Bb** and look black. The probability of a guinea pig in this litter being black is 1 or 100% – it is certain.

If a pig from this litter is bred with one from another litter from a similar cross, you can again calculate the chances of possible combinations of alleles and thus coat colours.

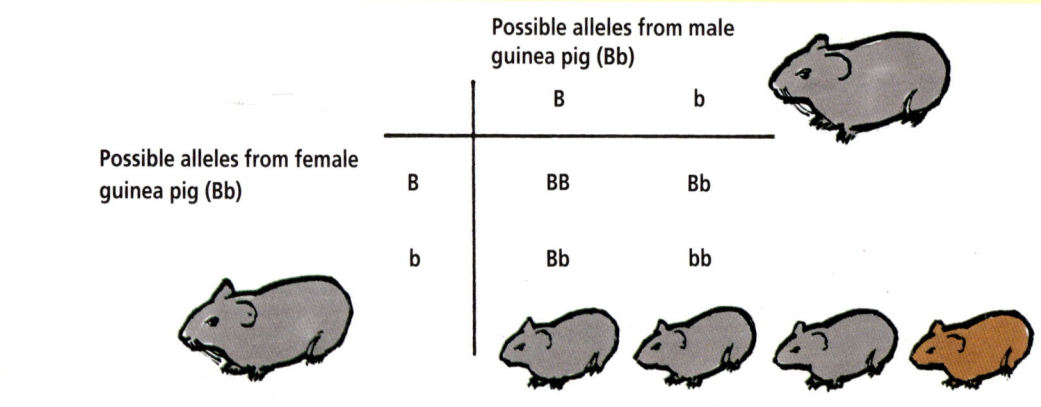

This time, there are four possible combinations of alleles. Two combinations result in **Bb**, one in **BB** and one in **bb**. So the probability of getting a brown guinea pig is 0.25 or 25% – a one-in-four chance.

As with all probabilities, the larger the litter, the more likely it is that the coat colours would agree with this calculated prediction.

5. Male or female?

The sex of humans is determined by genes carried on specific sex chromosomes. The sex chromosomes are easily identified and are referred to as the X and Y chromosomes. They carry different genes and look very different. Females have two X chromosomes while males have one X chromosome and one Y chromosome. Whether a child is male or female is determined by which sex chromosome is inherited from the father.

	Possible sex chromosomes inherited from the father	
	X	Y
X (from mother)	XX	XY
X (from mother)	XX	XY

Thus the possible chromosome combinations are two XX and two XY, giving an equal chance of a child being male or female.

No matter how many male and female children are in a family, there is always an equal chance of any new baby being male or female.

6. Why are more males colour blind than females?

The gene which controls red/green colour blindness in humans is carried on the X sex chromosome. Colour blindness is the recessive allele. Normal sight is the dominant allele.

Males have the sex chromosome combination XY. If they inherit the colour blindness allele on their X chromosome there is no dominant normal sight allele to mask it, as there is no corresponding gene on the Y chromosome. All males inheriting the colour blindness allele on their X chromosome are colour blind.

Females have the sex chromosome combination XX. If a female inherits only one colour blindness allele, she will not be colour blind as she also has the dominant normal sight allele to mask it. If a female inherits colour blindness alleles from both her parents then she will be colour blind. The chance of this happening is much lower than the chance of a male inheriting the allele from his mother.

7. What is the genetic code?

Chromosomes are made of the chemical DNA. A molecule of DNA has two strands and is shaped in the form of a double helix.

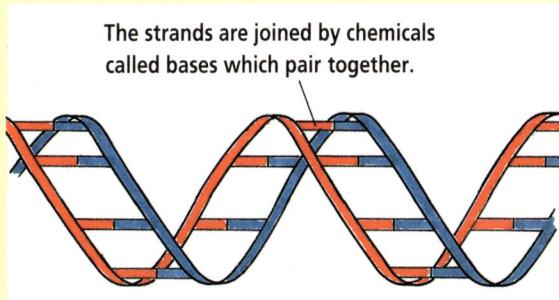

The strands are joined by chemicals called bases which pair together.

There are four different bases and it is the order of these bases along each DNA strand that determines what genes the chromosomes carry. The order of the bases is the **genetic code**.

What happens to the genetic code during chromosome replication?

The two strands in a molecule of DNA can separate and reform new partner strands. So two identical DNA molecules can be formed from one parent molecule. This is how chromosomes replicate during cell division (see *Thinking About 3* on page 29). The genetic code is not altered during this replication.

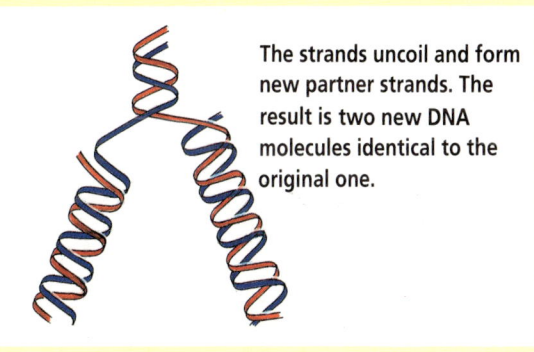

The strands uncoil and form new partner strands. The result is two new DNA molecules identical to the original one.

> **Taking it further**
> **How the genetic code is expressed**
> Genes consist of sections of chromosomes. Each gene has a particular DNA base sequence. Particular sequences of bases code for specific **amino acids**.
>
> Proteins are made of amino acids. Enzymes are proteins and so are also made of amino acids. All the different proteins and enzymes in your body have different amino acid sequences. These sequences are determined by the genetic code – the sequence of bases in the DNA in your chromosomes.
>
> Your cell reactions are controlled by enzymes, so the genetic code ultimately controls all the reactions which go on inside your body.

8. What is genetic engineering?

Genetic engineering means altering an organism's DNA so that its genetic code, and as a result the proteins it makes, are changed.

Bacteria are used in genetic engineering for two reasons:
- They have **plasmids**. These are circular structures made of DNA which control what proteins are made by the bacterium, but they are separate from the bacterium's chromosomes. Plasmids are independent of the rest of the cell so can be taken out of and put into a cell more easily than a chromosome.
- Bacteria reproduce very quickly in the right conditions, producing large numbers of genetically identical cells (**clones**).

The diagram shows how human insulin is produced by genetic engineering.

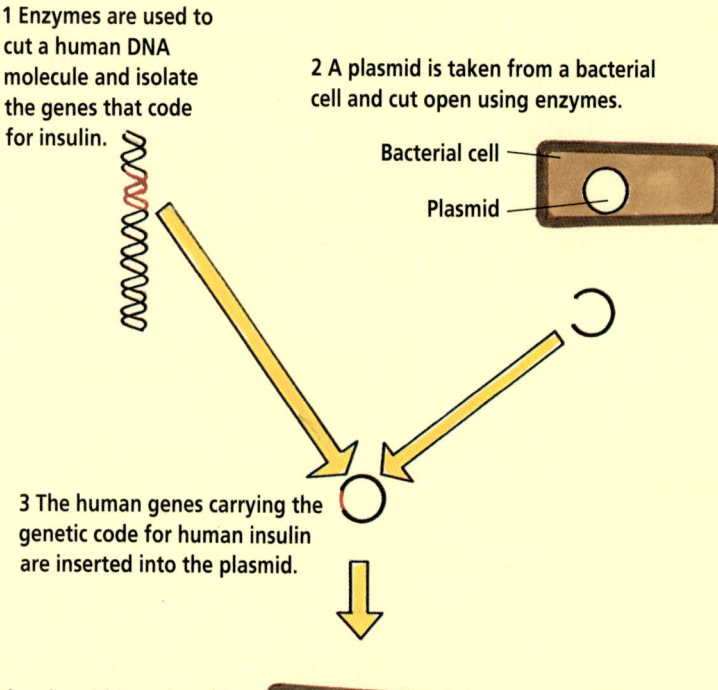

1 Enzymes are used to cut a human DNA molecule and isolate the genes that code for insulin.

2 A plasmid is taken from a bacterial cell and cut open using enzymes.

3 The human genes carrying the genetic code for human insulin are inserted into the plasmid.

4 The plasmid is replaced in a bacterial cell.

5 The bacterium is cultured (placed in conditions to encourage reproduction). Many clones (genetically identical cells) result.

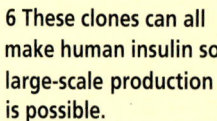

6 These clones can all make human insulin so large-scale production is possible.

Things to do

Evolution

Things to try out

1 Using flower wire or pipe cleaners try to make a simple model of DNA.

2 Find two counters. Let one counter represent the possible sex chromosomes from a mother. Mark both sides of this counter with an X. Let the other counter represent the possible sex chromosomes from a father. Mark one side of this counter with an X and the other side with a Y. Toss both counters and record whether they come down XX or XY. Do this several times. How many boys and girls do you get?

Things to find out

3 Apart from Darwin's finches, what other unusual animals are found on the Galapagos Islands?

4 Jean Baptiste de Lamarck proposed a theory of evolution long before Darwin and Wallace. What was Lamarck's theory and why is it not accepted?

5 Find out what James Watson and Francis Crick contributed to our understanding of DNA.

Points to discuss

6 In some school districts of the USA equal teaching time must be given to the theory of evolution by natural selection and the theory of special creation. Discuss whether you think this should be done in Britain.

7 'Experiments with genetic engineering are too dangerous and should be stopped.' Do you agree? Discuss the dangers of genetic engineering experiments.

Things to write about

8 Write an explanation of why parents with black hair may have children with red hair.

9 Your aunt and uncle in Australia have decided that they want two children; one girl and one boy. They have written to say that because their first child was a boy, their next child will be a girl. Write a reply.

10 'Chromosomes are the threads of life.' Write an explanation of what this means.

11 Imagine it is 1858 and you have just received a letter from Alfred Russel Wallace which explains the theory of evolution by natural selection – a theory which you have spent 25 years researching! Write a reply.

Questions to answer

(*Thinking About 5 and 6* will help you to answer these questions.)

12 If a red/green colour blind man marries a normal sighted woman with no history of colour blindness in her family, what is the risk of
(**a**) any of their sons being colour blind
(**b**) any of their daughters being colour blind?

13 Haemophilia is a medical disorder. People with haemophilia bleed easily and this bleeding can be difficult to stop. The allele for haemophilia is carried on the X sex chromosome. Why are most haemophilia sufferers men?

14

In mice, black coat colour is dominant to brown. If a pure-bred black mouse was mated with a pure-bred brown mouse, how many brown mice would you expect to get for every black one in the first generation? Explain your answer.

15 A cross of a pure-bred black mouse and a pure-bred brown mouse produced a black mouse. If that black mouse was mated with a pure-bred brown mouse, what proportion of black and brown mice would you expect to get?

16

Red and white are co-dominant alleles of coat colour in shorthorn cattle. Calves of a pure-bred red and pure-bred white cross are roan in appearance. What is the chance of a calf from a cross between a roan cow and a roan bull being
(**a**) red (**b**) white (**c**) roan?

17 Which of the chromosomes shown below make up homologous pairs?

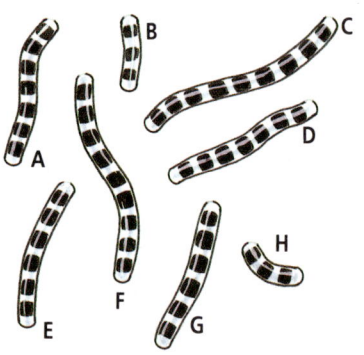

18 The allele (**R**) for the ability to tongue roll is dominant over the allele (**r**) for the inability to tongue roll. What tongue rolling alleles have each of the following?

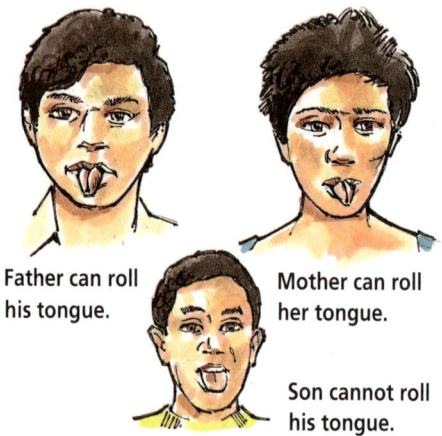

Father can roll his tongue.

Mother can roll her tongue.

Son cannot roll his tongue.

19 When breeding new plant varieties, the stamens of a plant being cross-pollinated are removed. Why is this done?

Introducing SPORTS SCIENCE

WORLD RECORDS (Women)									
Event	1950	1955	1960	1965	1970	1975	1980	1985	1990
100 m [1] (in seconds)	11.5	11.3	11.3	11.1	11.08	11.07	10.88	10.76	10.49
High jump (in metres)	1.71	1.73	1.86	1.91	1.91	1.95	2.01	2.07	2.09
Javelin [2] (in metres)	53.41	55.48	59.55	62.40	62.40	67.22	70.80	75.40	80.00

WORLD RECORDS (Men)									
Event	1950	1955	1960	1965	1970	1975	1980	1985	1990
100 m [1] (in seconds)	10.2	10.2	10.0	10.0	9.95	9.93	9.93	9.93	9.92
High jump (in metres)	2.11	2.12	2.22	2.28	2.28	2.30	2.36	2.41	2.44
Javelin [2] (in metres)	78.70	81.75	86.04	91.92	92.70	94.08	96.72	99.72	89.58

Notes: (1) More accurate timing for the 100 m was used from 1970.
(2) Javelin design altered in 1986 to protect spectators. In 1991 another change in design is being considered as throws of over 100 m are becoming a possibility with the new javelin.

1 Why do athletes keep on breaking records? Is it because the human race is getting stronger and fitter? Make a list of factors that could improve performance, such as changes in diet.

The Fosbury flop
One factor that can improve results is an advance in technique. The Fosbury flop is a technique used by high jumpers which improved performance dramatically.

Work, power and fitness
Technique alone is not enough to break records – you need power and fitness too.

Can you think of a scientific explanation of why the Fosbury flop gave better results than the straddle jump which it replaced?

2 Look at the photo at the bottom of the page. Write down
- why you would be doing work if you did this exercise
- how you could compare people's power during this exercise
- how you could measure their fitness using this exercise.

Do you find press-ups hard work?

IN THIS CHAPTER YOU WILL FIND OUT
- about work and power, and how you can measure them
- about methods of assessing your fitness
- how your muscles exert forces and enable you to move
- about gravitational potential energy and kinetic energy, and how you can calculate them
- about the behaviour of levers, balancing objects and stability.

Looking at

LOOKING AT: SPORTS SCIENCE

Jumping and Vaulting

Aiming high
The aim of high jumpers and pole vaulters is to get as high as possible. They both need to gain as much gravitational potential energy as possible. They do this in different ways.

Pole vaulters sprint towards the bar and then try to convert as much of their kinetic energy as possible into potential energy. In contrast, most high jumpers run quite slowly towards the bar. It is difficult for them to convert horizontal running motion into extra jump height. Instead, jumpers look for ways of getting over the bar which raise their centre of mass as little as possible.

Centre of mass
Your body behaves as though all its mass were centred at one point – your **centre of mass**. There is more about this in *Thinking About 8* on pages 45-6.

Your centre of mass standing upright or lying flat is roughly in the middle of your body – perhaps slightly nearer your head, if your upper body is heavier than your legs.

1. These diagrams are part of an explanation of how to find the exact position of someone's centre of mass when lying flat. Write a set of instructions to go with the diagrams. Explain how to do the measurement and how to calculate how far the centre of mass is above the feet. *Thinking About 7* on page 44 will help.

$h \times F_1 = 2.00 \times F_2$

High jumping
The world high jump record is around 2.0 m for women and 2.3 m for men. The centre of mass of a woman is on average about 1 m above the ground and that of a man about 1.3 m above the ground. So you can see that in both cases they have to raise their centre of mass by 1 m to clear these heights.

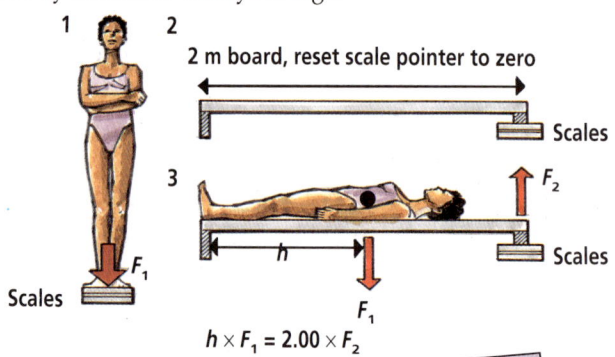

In the straddle jumping style, the jumper is almost flat when crossing the bar. Her centre of mass is perhaps 15 cm above the bar.

2. In the Fosbury flop, the jumper bends backwards to cross the bar. In a successful jump, the jumper's centre of mass may not even get as high as the bar! Use the diagram of the centre of mass of a curved shape in *Thinking About 8* on page 45 to explain clearly how this is possible.

In the 1960s, the American Dick Fosbury invented a new jumping style, the Fosbury flop. He won the Olympic gold medal in 1968. Almost all the top jumpers now use the Fosbury flop method.

LOOKING AT: SPORTS SCIENCE

Pole vaulting

A pole vaulter runs as fast as possible towards the bar, plants his pole in the socket and uses his forward speed to bend the pole. At the same time he pulls downwards with his arms to flex the pole even more.

Imagine that his speed is almost equal to that of a top sprinter, say 9.5 m/s, and that *all* his kinetic energy is converted into potential energy. How high can he vault?

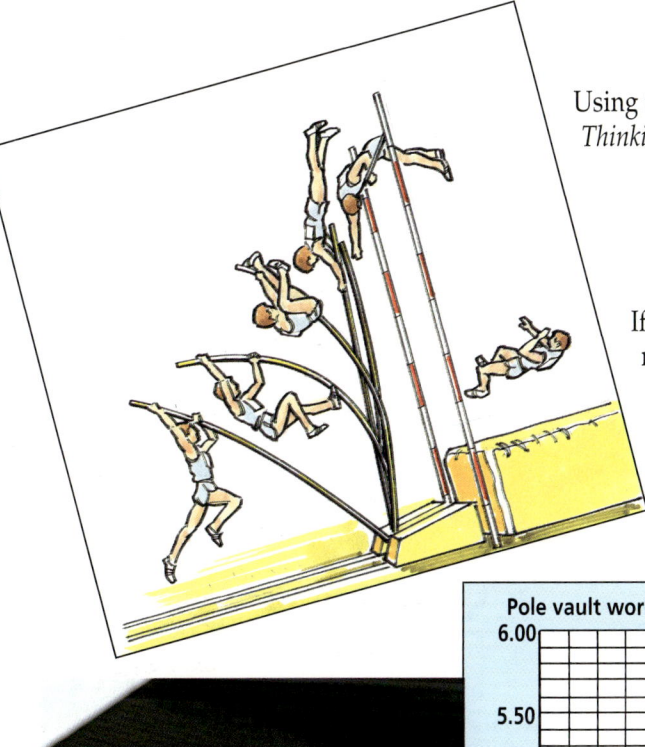

final potential energy = original kinetic energy

Using the equations for potential and kinetic energy (from *Thinking About 5* on page 42):

$$mgh = \tfrac{1}{2}mv^2$$
$$10 \times h = \tfrac{1}{2}(9.5)^2$$
So, $h = 4.5$ metres

If his centre of mass is 1.3 metres above the ground when running, he might clear a bar $4.5 + 1.3 = 5.8$ m high. This is remarkably close to the current (1991) world record, 6.10 m.

But the calculation is not accurate – it is largely chance that the answer is so close to reality. There are two errors which cancel each other out:

- The vaulter cannot convert *all* his kinetic energy into potential energy – some energy is used in flexing the pole.
- But the pole stores *more* potential energy because he pulls down on it, flexing it further. As it straightens, it pushes him upwards.

The potential energy stored in the pole depends on how flexible it is, and that depends on the material it is made from. Pole vaulters nowadays use glass fibre poles, which were first introduced in the late 1960s. You can see their effect on the world record graph.

Pole vault world record (men)

3 Use the information above to write a paragraph describing and explaining how the men's world pole vaulting record has improved since 1900.

4 Pole vaulters are even better than Fosbury floppers at getting over the bar without raising their centre of mass any more than necessary. Use a cardboard model and *Thinking About 8* on page 45 to estimate the position of the centre of mass of the vaulter in the diagram as he goes over the bar.

In brief

Sports Science

1. Most sports involve using your muscles to do physical **work**. Scientists use a very precise definition of work. Work is done when a force makes an object move.

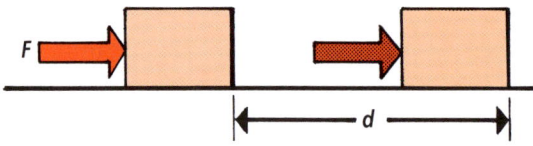

The amount of work is calculated from the equation:

$$\text{work} = \text{force} \times \text{distance}$$
$$w = Fd$$

The distance must be measured in the direction of the force.

2. The units of work are **newton metres**, which are also called **joules (J)**. One joule is the amount of work done by a force of one newton when it moves an object a distance of one metre.

3. When a force does work, it transfers **energy** from one form to another. The amount of work done is equal to the amount of energy transferred. Like work, energy is also measured in joules.

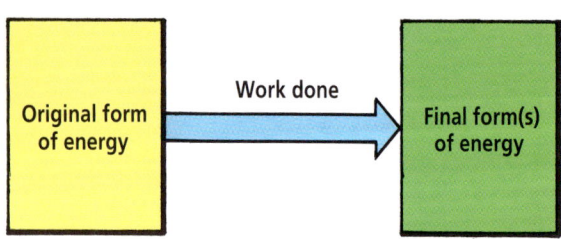

4. **Power** is the rate at which a person or a machine can do work:

$$\text{power} = \frac{\text{work done}}{\text{time taken}}$$

Power can also be defined as the rate at which energy is transferred in the process:

$$\text{power} = \frac{\text{energy transferred}}{\text{time taken}}$$

5. Power is measured in **watts (W)**. One watt is one joule per second. Larger powers are measured in kilowatts (kW) or megawatts (MW). 1 kilowatt is 1000 watts; 1 megawatt is 1 000 000 watts.

6. Fitness tests may involve measuring:
   - the power of certain muscles
   - the time you take to recover after exercise.

7. When you exercise, a chemical reaction takes place in your muscles. Glucose and oxygen are used up and carbon dioxide, water and lactic acid are produced. Work is done and heat is also produced.

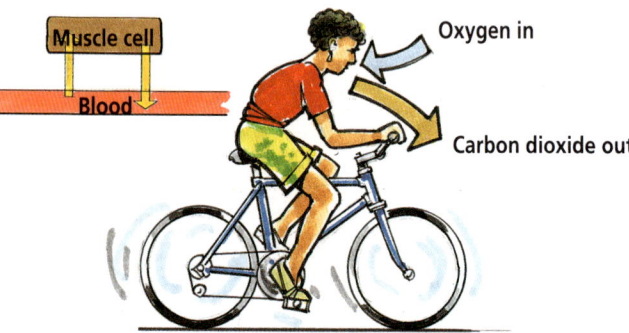

8. When you lift an object, you increase its **gravitational potential energy**.

The gain in gravitational potential energy is calculated by the equation:

$$E_p = mgh$$

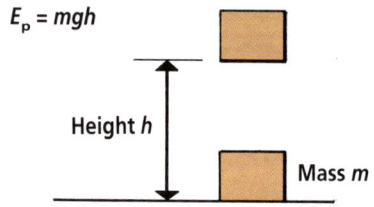

9. Any moving object has **kinetic energy**.

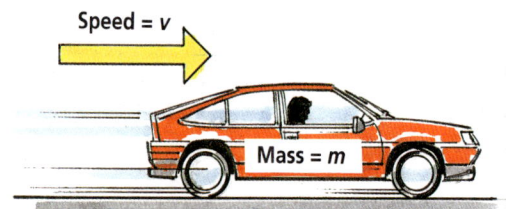

The amount of kinetic energy depends on the mass of the object and its speed:

$$E_k = \tfrac{1}{2}mv^2$$

IN BRIEF: SPORTS SCIENCE

10 If an object slides or rolls down a slope, it loses gravitational potential energy and gains kinetic energy. If there is no friction, the amount of kinetic energy it gains is *equal* to the amount of gravitational potential energy it has lost.

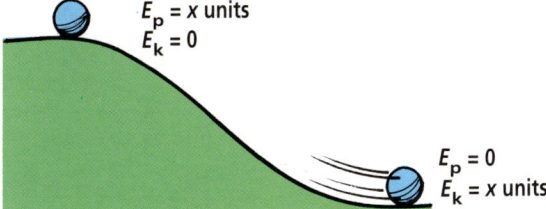

This means that the ball's speed at the bottom of the hill does not depend on the shape of the slope, but only on the drop in height.

The same is true in the other direction. If an object slides or rolls up a slope, it loses kinetic energy and gains gravitational potential energy. If there is no friction, the amount of gravitational potential energy it gains is equal to the amount of kinetic energy it loses.

11 **Muscles** exert forces by contracting. In vertebrates, muscles are attached to the bones of the skeleton and operate joints like a system of levers.

Most joints are moved by a pair of muscles, one moving the joint in one direction and the other moving it back.

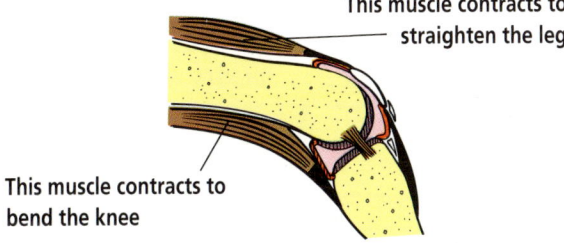

12 The **turning effect** of a force is calculated by the equation:

turning effect = force × distance from pivot

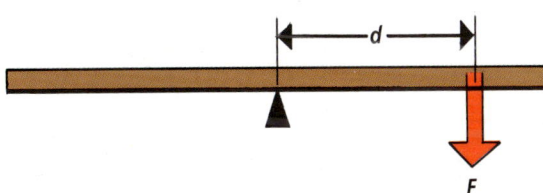

The distance is measured *at right angles* to the direction of the force. (Notice how this is different from the equation for work in *In Brief 1*.)

13 An object **balances** if the total turning effect in the clockwise direction is equal to the total turning effect in the anticlockwise direction.

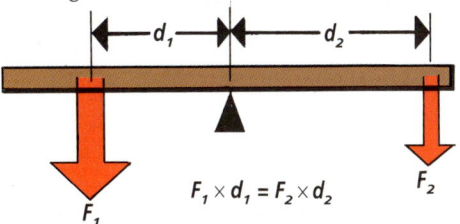

$$F_1 \times d_1 = F_2 \times d_2$$

14 You can use **levers** to move something more easily. Some levers multiply the *force* you apply. The force you apply is smaller than the load. But the load moves a shorter distance than the applied force.

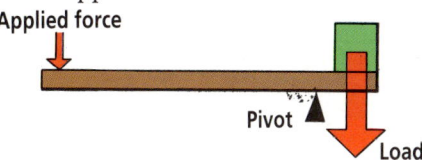

Using a teaspoon to open a tin of syrup is an example of this kind of lever.

Other levers are used to multiply the *distance* the applied force moves. The force you apply moves a short distance and makes the load move a longer distance. But the applied force has to be bigger than the load.

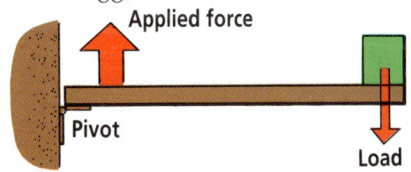

Lifting a weight in your hand with your forearm outstretched is an example of this kind of lever.

15 Every object behaves as if all its mass were concentrated at a single point called the **centre of mass**. When an object hangs, its centre of mass is always directly below the point of suspension.

16 An object is **stable** if its centre of mass is low, or if it has a wide base. You have to tip it a long way to push its centre of mass past the edge it is pivoting on.

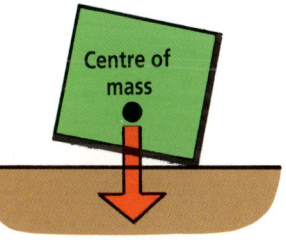

Thinking about
Sports Science

1. What is work?

If you are keen on sport you will know that many sports involve doing physical work – and feeling very tired afterwards. The people in these photographs are making their muscles work hard.

In everyday life we also use the word 'work' to describe other, less physically strenuous activities.

For these people, work means operating a computer terminal.

A long homework task feels like hard work.

In science we use the word **work** with a clearly defined meaning. Work is done when a force makes something move through a certain distance. The amount of work involved is calculated by multiplying the force (in newtons) by the distance the object moves in the direction of the force (in metres):

work = force × distance

The units of work are **newton metres**, or **joules** (J). One newton metre is the same thing as one joule.

Notice that work, in the scientific sense, is only done when the force actually makes something move.

Tug-of-war: no movement, no work being done

One team starts to move: work now being done

Holding weights still: no work being done

Raising weights: work now being done

Work and energy

Work = force × distance is a useful definition in science. When a force does work, it transfers energy from one form to another. The amount of work done is equal to the amount of energy transferred. Look at these examples.

Pushing sled – sled speeding up

A bob-sled on ice is very smooth running. Even so, you have to apply a force to start it moving. The force moves the sled a certain distance and so work is done.

The amount of work done is equal to the amount of chemical energy the crewman's muscles have converted to kinetic energy in the sled.

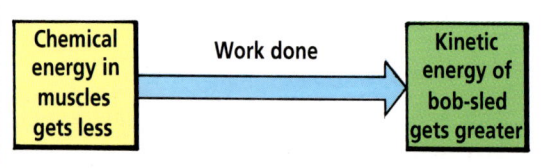

Chemical energy in muscles gets less → Work done → Kinetic energy of bob-sled gets greater

When an athlete lifts a loaded bar above his head, he applies an upward force. The force moves the weights a certain distance and so work is done.

The amount of work done is again equal to the amount of chemical energy the athlete's muscles have converted to gravitational potential energy.

Pushing upwards on weights – weights gaining height

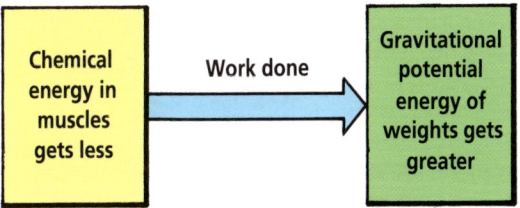

Work can be done by machines as well as by people. In this case, the work done is equal to the amount of chemical energy in the fuel converted to kinetic or potential energy.

2. How powerful are you?

You might describe the sprinters and oarsman on the opposite page as 'powerful'. But what does 'power' mean?

Power is the rate at which a person or a machine can do work – or can transfer energy from one form to another. Imagine that a pile of bricks have to be loaded on to the back of a truck. A person who is powerful can do the work in a shorter time than a less powerful person.

Power (in watts) is the amount of work (in joules) done in each second:

$$\text{power} = \frac{\text{work done}}{\text{time taken}}$$

Or you can think of power as the amount of energy transferred each second:

$$\text{power} = \frac{\text{energy transferred}}{\text{time taken}}$$

Both definitions amount to the same thing. One watt is equal to one joule per second.

3. What is fitness?

There are two aspects of **fitness**. One is the ability to perform certain physical tasks. The second is the speed with which you recover after an activity. Various fitness tests can be used to estimate both aspects of fitness.

Measuring your power

Some fitness tests begin by measuring the power of different muscles. Here is a way of doing this for your leg muscles.

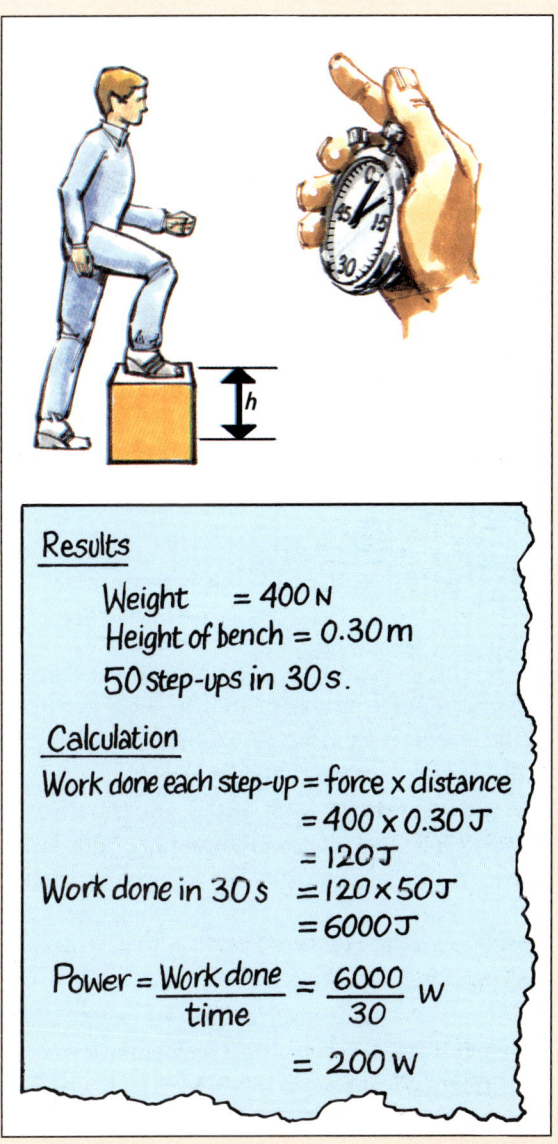

Things to Do 1 on page 46 gives details of another fitness test which measures your recovery time.

4. What causes the changes in your body after exercise?

When you do strenuous exercise, several changes happen in your body:

- you breathe more quickly and deeply
- your heart beats faster
- your skin temperature rises and you sweat to help you cool down
- your muscles ache.

In order to do work, muscles must contract. The contraction process involves chemical changes inside the muscle fibres. Glucose (from food) and oxygen (from the air you breathe in) are brought to your muscles by your blood. They take part in the reaction which enables the muscle to contract.

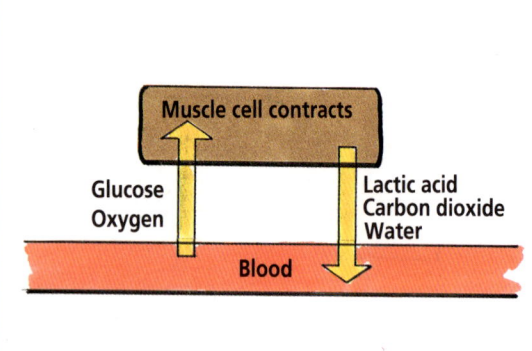

Work is done when a muscle contracts and energy is released in the form of heat. The waste products of the reaction include carbon dioxide and lactic acid. These are carried away by the blood.

When you exercise, your muscles do extra work. So you need more glucose and oxygen. Your heart rate increases, to pump glucose and oxygen more quickly to your muscles. Your breathing rate increases for the same reason – to get more oxygen into the blood.

The reaction in the muscles releases energy as heat and this raises your body temperature. Sweating is a response to this; the evaporation of sweat helps cool you down.

The tired ache you feel after exercise is due partly to the build-up of lactic acid in your muscles. This takes some time to be carried away by the blood.

5. How can we calculate amounts of kinetic energy and potential energy?

When a high jumper springs upwards to try to clear the bar, he is using his muscles to do work. He wants to gain enough gravitational potential energy to clear the bar.

When a sprinter pushes off from the starting blocks, she is using her muscles to do the work. She wants to increase her kinetic energy as quickly as possible.

You can use the ideas about work in *Thinking About 1* to help you calculate amounts of gravitational potential energy and kinetic energy.

Gravitational potential energy

Imagine lifting a box of mass m kilograms through a vertical height of h metres.

Weight of box = mg newtons (where g is 10 N/kg, the strength of the Earth's gravitational field).
So the upward force to lift the box = mg newtons.

work done = force × distance moved
= $mg \times h$ joules

The amount of work done is the same as the amount of gravitational potential energy gained by the box: mgh joules.

$$E_p = mgh$$

Kinetic energy

The equation for kinetic energy is not so easy to derive. The equation is:

$$E_k = \tfrac{1}{2}mv^2$$

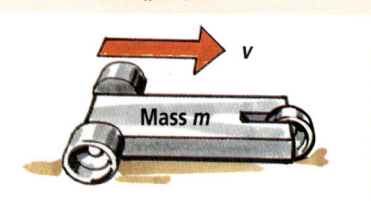

6. How can we use the potential energy and kinetic energy equations?

Water slide
This water chute is very smooth and slippery. The top is 5 metres higher than the bottom. A child of mass 30 kg slides down. What speed has she reached by the time she gets to the bottom?

The child has extra gravitational potential energy at the top. As she slides down, this is converted into kinetic energy. As the chute is smooth there is little or no friction. So the amount of kinetic energy she has at the bottom will be exactly the same as the potential energy she had at the top.

amount of extra E_p at top = mgh
$= 30 \times 10 \times 5$ joules
$= 1500$ joules

So she has 1500 J of kinetic energy at the bottom. From this we can work out her speed:

$$E_k = \tfrac{1}{2}mv^2$$
$$1500 = \tfrac{1}{2} \times 30 \times v^2$$
So: $v^2 = 2 \times \dfrac{1500}{30} = 100$
$$v = 10 \text{ m/s}$$

Bowling
At a ten-pin bowling alley, the returning bowls run along a channel beside the lane and up a little ramp into a storage area. The bowls roll back at a speed of 2 m/s. If you were designing a rink, how high could you make the storage area? (A bowl has a mass of 3 kg.)

The bowl has kinetic energy as it rolls back along the channel. As it rises up the ramp, this is converted into gravitational potential energy. The amount of kinetic energy is fixed by the mass and speed of the bowl. So there is a limit to the amount of potential energy it can gain. This limits the height of ramp it can get up.

The returning bowl has $E_k = \tfrac{1}{2}mv^2$
$= \tfrac{1}{2} \times 3 \times 2^2$
$= 6$ joules

So the maximum amount of potential energy it can gain is 6 joules.

So: $E_p = mgh$
$6 = 3 \times 10 \times h$

Rearranging this: $h = \tfrac{6}{30}$ m $= 0.2$ m

So the ramp must be no more than 0.2 m (20 cm) high.

The important thing about both these calculations is that the shape of the chute and ramp doesn't matter – just the vertical height of the drop or rise. This makes the potential and kinetic energy equations very useful. However, the friction has to be small. If there is a lot of friction, some of the original energy is lost in the form of heat. It is not all transferred from kinetic energy to potential energy, or vice versa. But if these energy losses are small enough to ignore, the method is very useful.

7. How do people move?

Muscles can only exert forces by **contracting** – getting shorter. They pull on bones to make you move. The skeleton acts as a system of levers, operated by the pulls of pairs of muscles. The diagram shows the pair of muscles in your upper arm.

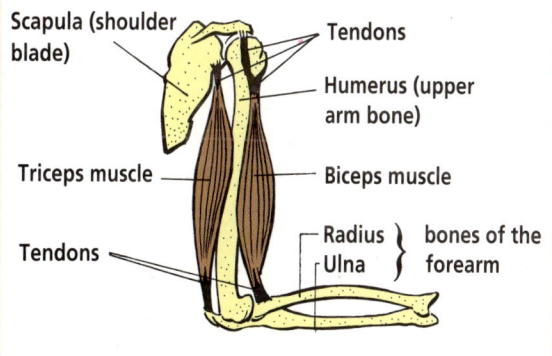

The elbow joint is flexed (moved) by the **biceps** and **triceps** muscles. The top ends of these muscles are connected to the bones of the shoulder. The lower end of the biceps is connected to the upper bone of your forearm and the triceps to the lower one. To bend the arm, the biceps contracts and the triceps relaxes. To straighten it again, the triceps contracts and the biceps relaxes and allows itself to be stretched again. The muscles cannot push, they can only pull.

The law of the lever: a quick reminder

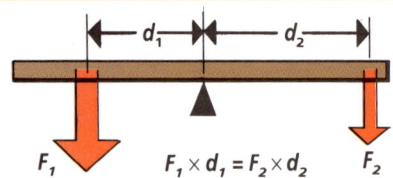

A simple lever has its pivot in the middle. The turning effect of a force is calculated by the equation:

turning effect = force × distance from pivot

The lever **balances** if the turning effects in both directions are the same. If one is bigger than the other, the lever will turn that way.

You can have more than one load on each side. You just work out the turning effects of all the forces turning the lever in the same direction and add them.

You can use a lever to *multiply* the *force* you exert. If you exert a small force a long way from the pivot, this can overcome a much larger force closer to the pivot.

This lever multiplies the force exerted by the hand.

You can also use a lever to *multiply* the *distance* a force moves. If you exert a force close to the pivot, the end of the lever will move a longer distance than the force moves.

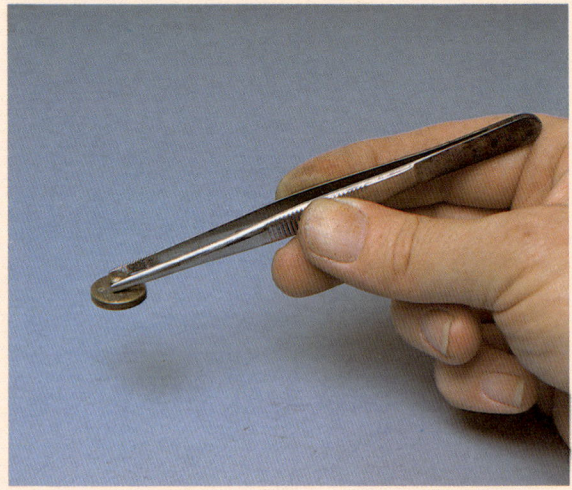

This lever multiplies the distance moved by the fingers.

The elbow joint as a lever system
This simplified model shows how the elbow bends.

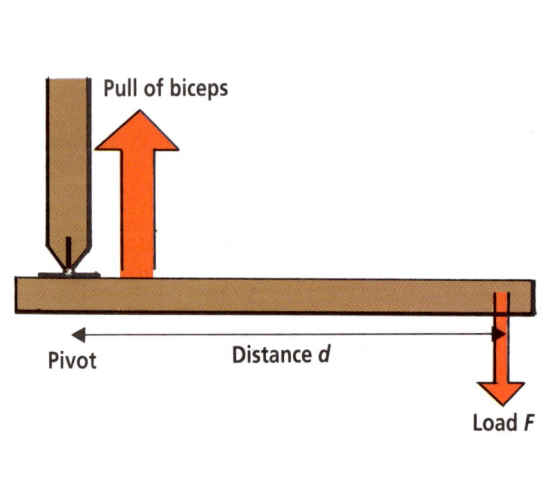

A weight in the hand is further from the pivot than the biceps force, so it has a bigger turning effect (Fd). The biceps force has to be bigger than the force exerted by the load. But the advantage of this sort of lever is that a small contraction of the biceps can move the hand through quite a large distance.

THINKING ABOUT: SPORTS SCIENCE

8. How do things balance?

Imagine hanging up a metre ruler by a thread. If the thread is in the middle, it will balance. The turning effect of the right-hand end of the ruler is equal to the turning effect of the left-hand end.

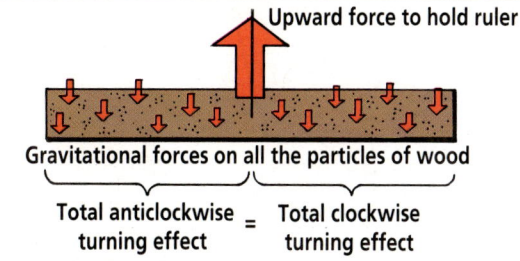

The ruler behaves as if all its mass were concentrated at its mid-point, so that no turning effect is produced.

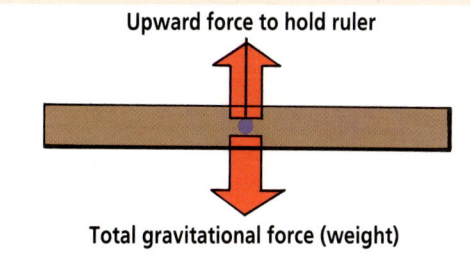

Imagine doing the same thing with a tapering wooden bar. This would also balance at some point, though not in the middle. At the balance point, the turning effect of the wood on the right-hand side is equal to the turning effect of the wood on the left-hand side.

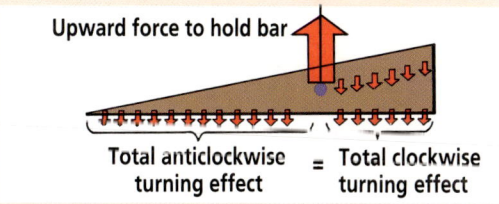

Again it behaves as if its mass were all concentrated at one point. This point is called the **centre of mass**. Every object has a centre of mass.

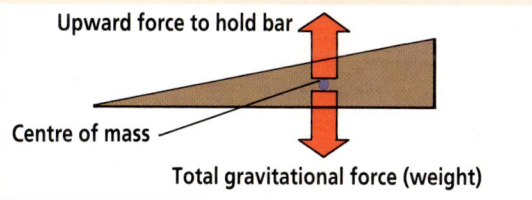

You can find the position of the centre of mass of an object by hanging it up from two different points. The centre of mass is always directly below the point of suspension. It must be where the two lines PQ and XY cross.

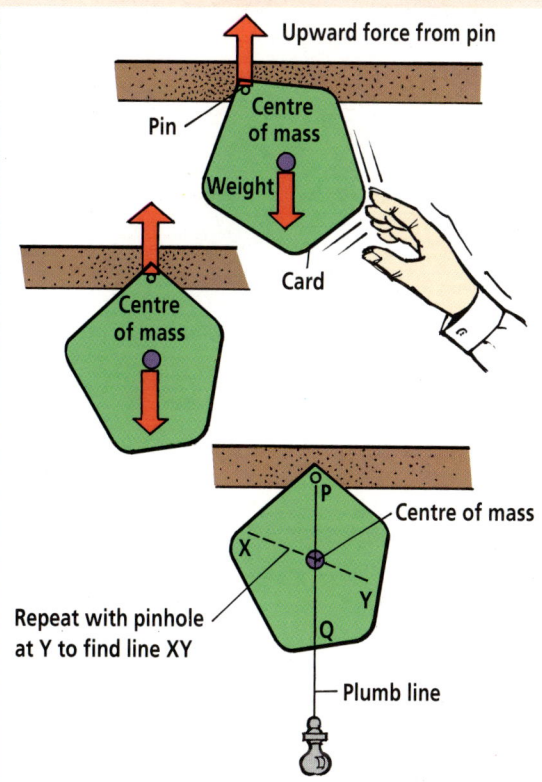

For some shapes, the centre of mass may not actually be a point *on* the body at all.

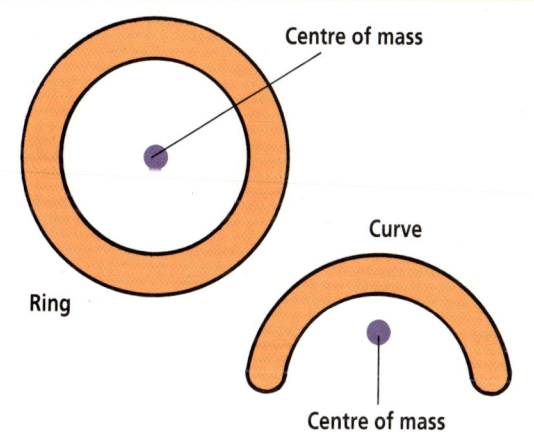

Looking at Jumping and Vaulting on pages 36–7 shows how centre of mass can be important in some sports.

Centre of mass and stability

The position of the centre of mass determines whether an object is easy or difficult to topple over. An object topples if you push its centre of mass beyond the edge of its base.

Box returns to original position.

Box topples over.

This box is just on the point of tipping over.

A broader base makes the box more stable.

A heavy base lowers the centre of gravity so the box does not tip over so easily.

Objects can be designed to be very stable.

Testing the stability of a bus. Its low centre of mass makes it very stable. Here you can see that it tips a long way without falling over.

The legs of a child's high chair are splayed outwards so that the base is wide. This makes the chair very stable.

Things to do

Sports Science

Things to try out

1 *Thinking About 4* on page 42 describes what happens to your body when you exercise. Your **recovery time** is the time it takes for these things to return to normal. Recovery time and power of muscles (see *Thinking About 3*) are important measures of fitness. These ideas are combined in the Harvard Step Test, which lets you measure your 'fitness index'. Try it.

This is what you have to do:

(a) Find a bench or box 0.5 m high.
(b) Step up and down at a rate of one step every 2 s for 5 minutes.
(c) Rest for 1 minute.
(d) Get a friend to count your pulse for 30 s.
(e) Rest for 30 s, then count your pulse for 30 s again.
(f) Rest for another 30 s, then count your pulse for 30 s for a third time.

(g) Work out your 'fitness index' like this:

Time of exercise = 300 s

Multiply by 100: 30 000 – this is (A)

First pulse count =   _____
Second pulse count =   _____
Third pulse count =   _____

Add the three pulse counts: _____

Multiply this number by 2 – this is (B)

Divide A by B – this is your 'fitness index'. The higher your index, the fitter you are:

50–59	60–69	70–79	80–90	over 90
poor	fair	good	excellent	superb

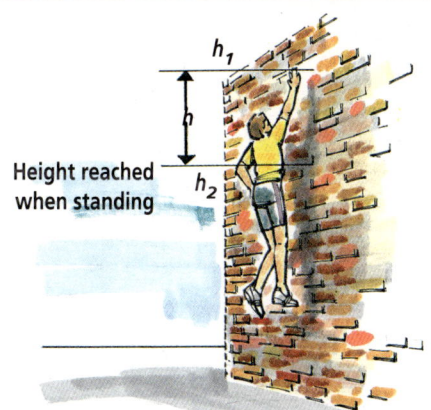

2 (a) How high can you jump from a standing start? You can measure this by marking the highest point you can reach on a wall when you jump. Then measure how far this is above the highest point you can touch while standing on the ground.
(b) Now use bathroom scales to find your mass in kilograms. Calculate how much gravitational potential energy you have gained at the highest point of your jump. (The equation you need is in *Thinking About 5* on page 42.)
(c) The height you can jump depends on how fast you are moving as you leave the ground. From your answer to part **(b)**, you can work out your kinetic energy at the moment you left the ground. Use this to calculate your take-off speed. (Again the equation you need is in *Thinking About 5*.)

3 Use a ticker timer to make a record of the motion of a sprinter over the first five metres of a run. Use your tape to work out the sprinter's average speed during each half-second of the run. Draw a graph to summarize these results. Write a paragraph to explain why your graph has the shape it has.

Things to find out

4 Use the reference section of your school library to find out how the world record for the 200 metres (for men and women) has improved since 1900. Draw two graphs to show the changes in the record. Do you think there is a limit to how fast a person can run 200 m? Do your graphs suggest that there is a limit?

Things to write about

5 Jane has cereal and milk, toast and a glass of orange juice for breakfast. She then cycles to school. Her route first goes up a steep hill, then she freewheels down the other side and along a level road to school. Write a paragraph describing all the energy changes which take place.

6 Your uncle has a table lamp made from a bottle. Unfortunately he finds that it keeps toppling over. Write to him explaining how he could make it more stable by partly filling it with sand. Explain to him (in simple language) the science behind this.

Points to discuss

7 Public swimming pools and leisure centres are expensive to build and run. Discuss with others in your group whether you think that public sports facilities are a good use of taxpayers' money. Make a list of the arguments you would use to support the idea of public sports facilities in your local area.

Questions to answer

8 How much work do you do in the following situations?

(a) pushing a loaded supermarket trolley with a force of 80 N for a distance of 200 m

(b) pushing a drawer shut with a force of 6 N for a distance of 0.4 m

(c) lifting a suitcase of mass 15 kg on to a car roof-rack, 1.75 m above the ground

(d) holding an object of mass 5 kg steady at arm's length

9 A tourist (mass 70 kg) in London has a large cream bun with his coffee. Aware that this amounts to 1200 kJ, he decides to climb the stairs to the top of the Post Office Tower (170 m high) to work it off.

(a) How much work does he do in climbing the stairs?

(b) If muscles are 20% efficient (i.e. 20% of the energy in food is available as work; the rest is wasted as heating) how many kilojoules has he managed to work off?

(c) How many times would he need to go up the tower to work off the cream bun?

10 What is the gain or loss of gravitational potential energy in each of the following situations?

(a) a child of mass 25 kg climbs a 12 m flight of stairs

(b) a high jumper of mass 50 kg raises her centre of mass from 1.0 m (standing) to 1.75 m as she crosses the bar

(c) a high-board diver of mass 60 kg dives from a 5 m board into a pool.

11 According to the *Guinness Book of Records*, in 1979 James Rafferty ran up the Empire State Building in New York (a height of 362 m) in 12 minutes and 20 seconds. If his mass was 70 kg, what was his gain in gravitational potential energy in this time? What average power did he develop?

12 This graph shows how a sprinter's speed changes over the first 1.6 s of a run.

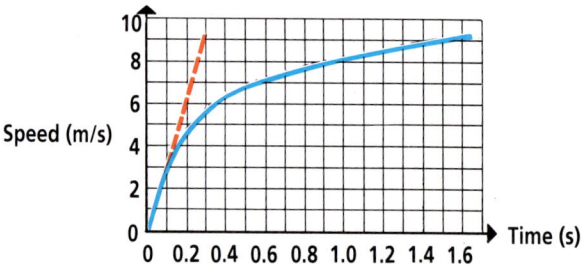

(a) Describe in detail the motion of the sprinter over this time.

(b) Estimate the sprinter's acceleration out of the blocks. (*Remember*: acceleration = change of speed/time taken. You need to estimate her change of speed over a short time at the start of the motion.)

(c) If the sprinter's mass is 45 kg, what force must she exert to achieve this initial acceleration? (*Hint*: $F = ma$.)

13 How much kinetic energy do the following moving objects possess?

(a) a bicycle and rider of total mass 85 kg, travelling at 15 m/s

(b) a volleyball of mass 0.8 kg, travelling at 3 m/s

(c) a long jumper of mass 55 kg, running at 6 m/s

14 A toy car is released from point A on a smooth track.

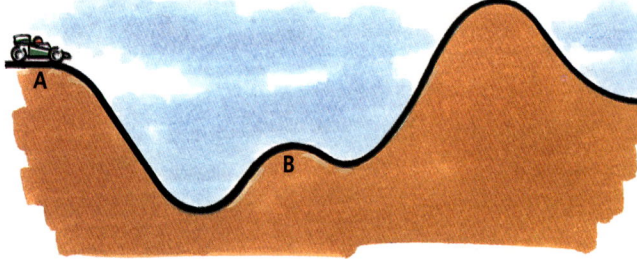

(a) Describe its motion between A and B. Use the terms *gravitational potential energy* and *kinetic energy* in your description.

(b) What is the furthest point the car will go on the track? Where will it finally stop? Explain your answers.

Introducing
BURNING AND BONDING

BURNING AND BONDING   49

Burning is a chemical change. The materials which are burning in this building are combining with oxygen to form new substances. But 'new substances' does not mean 'new atoms'. All the atoms that were in the materials before the fire are still there afterwards. All that happens is that the atoms which were bonded together become bonded to oxygen atoms instead.

Natural gas which is used for cooking and heating is mainly methane. When it burns it combines with oxygen and releases a lot of energy. You can see the light from the flame and the pan and milk are heated.

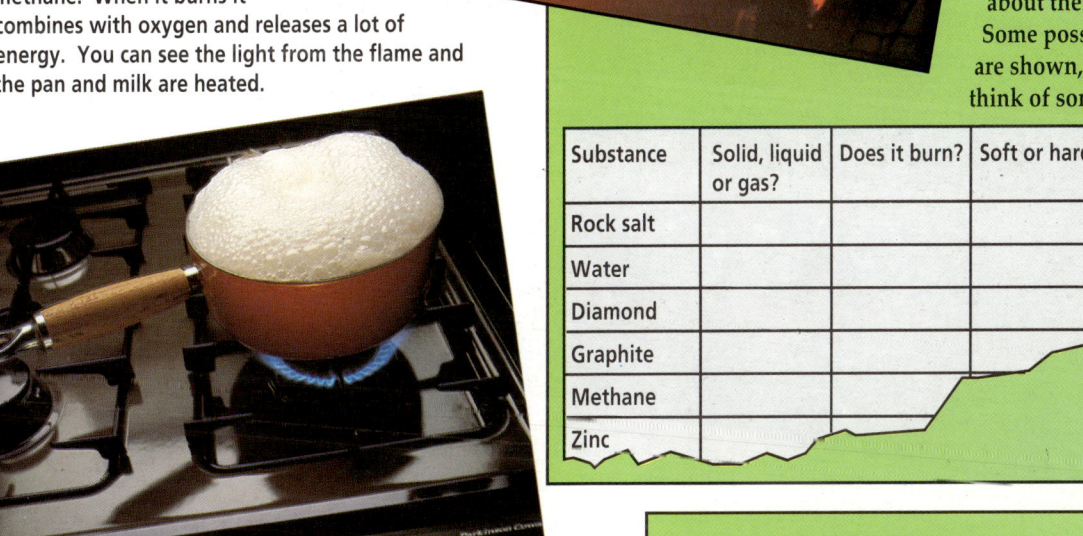

1 The table lists substances which will be discussed in this chapter. Draw your own table and record what you know about their properties. Some possible headings are shown, but you may think of some more.

Substance	Solid, liquid or gas?	Does it burn?	Soft or hard?	Does it conduct electricity?
Rock salt				
Water				
Diamond				
Graphite				
Methane				
Zinc				

Looking closely at what happens to substances when they burn provides important evidence about how the atoms are bonded together in those substances. We can use theories of bonding and structure to explain why different substances have different properties.

IN THIS CHAPTER YOU WILL FIND OUT
- how theories of bond breaking and bond making can explain the burning of a fuel
- about the use of liquid fuels in motor vehicles and their environmental consequences
- how theories about different types of bonding can explain differences in properties
- how similarities and trends in properties of elements can be related to their positions in the periodic table.

Looking at

Sir Humphrey Davy

LOOKING AT: BURNING AND BONDING

1 You have been asked to write the script for a radio programme about Humphrey Davy and his achievements. This Looking At provides some of the facts. You may need to dramatise parts to capture the listener's imagination.

DAVY'S LIFE

- 1778 ~ Born in Penzance, Cornwall
- 1785-95 ~ Educated at schools in Penzance and Truro
- 1798 ~ Appointed Chemical Superintendent of the Pneumatic Institute
- 1801 ~ Joined Royal Institute, London
- 1806 ~ Published *On some Chemical Agencies of Electricity*
- 1807 ~ Discovered sodium and potassium
- 1808 ~ Discovered the alkaline earth metals magnesium, calcium, strontium and barium
- 1812 ~ Married a rich widow
- 1812 ~ Was knighted
- 1813-15 ~ Toured Europe with his wife and Michael Faraday
- 1815 ~ Undertook a study of explosions for the Society for the Prevention of Accidents in Mines
- 1820 ~ Appointed President of the Royal Society
- 1827 ~ Resigned his post as President due to failing health
- 1829 ~ Died in Geneva, Switzerland

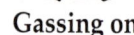

Gassing on

Davy's first job was as Chemical Superintendent of the Pneumatic Institute. Pneumatic means 'of the air', and the Institute was founded to study different gases.

Davy was an enthusiastic experimenter, who thought nothing of using people in experiments. He persuaded his friends Robert Southey and Samuel Taylor Coleridge (both famous poets) to inhale nitrous oxide. As it happened, this was not too risky, but Davy did not know this. One theory about nitrous oxide at the time was that it was responsible for causing disease!

When Davy tested nitrous oxide on himself he noticed that he could no longer feel his toothache. He had discovered the anaesthetic properties of the gas.

However, it was not until 50 years later that the gas was used when extracting teeth.

Davy took even more risks experimenting on himself by inhaling water gas. He nearly died as a result – which is not surprising when you realise that water gas is a mixture of steam and carbon monoxide.

Davy and Napoleon

Although England and France were at war for much of Davy's life, this did not greatly affect relationships between scientists in the two countries. Davy won the Napoleon prize in 1807 for his work *On some Chemical Agencies of Electricity*. In 1813, when Davy embarked on a two-year tour of Europe, Napoleon allowed him to move freely through France and the territories France had conquered.

Davy visited Napoleon's court and he and his wife were presented to the Emperor and Empress.

LOOKING AT: BURNING AND BONDING   51

Elementary discoveries

When Davy first began work at the Royal Institute, he concentrated on the new subject of electro-chemistry. A device to produce an electric current, the first electric cell, had recently been invented. It was called Volta's pile, and was made of alternate zinc and silver disks, separated by damp paper.

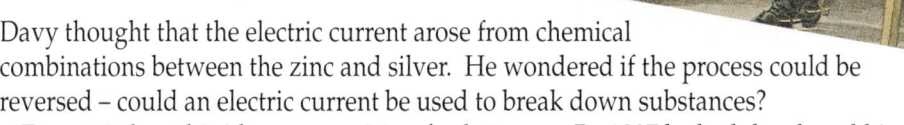

Davy thought that the electric current arose from chemical combinations between the zinc and silver. He wondered if the process could be reversed – could an electric current be used to break down substances?

Davy tried out his idea on a variety of substances. By 1807 he had developed his method sufficiently to be able to decompose soda and potash (sodium carbonate and potassium carbonate). He called the soft silvery metals that he obtained 'sodium' and 'potassium'.

The following year he discovered strontium and barium, and then magnesium and calcium. In two years he had discovered six new elements!

The Davy lamp

Davy is most famous for inventing the Davy safety lamp. It was the result of research that he carried out for the Society for the Prevention of Accidents in Mines.

A gas called firedamp (now known as methane) builds up in coal mines. Miners used naked candles to work by, and the candles sometimes ignited pockets of firedamp, causing explosions. They could not cover the candles with glass because a flame needs oxygen to burn.

Davy discovered that firedamp only ignited above a certain temperature. He filled a narrow metal tube with firedamp and found that an explosion would not pass through it. This gave him an idea for a design for a lamp.

He developed a lamp which had a double layer of metal gauze around the flame. The gauze let the air in so the flame would continue to burn. It also let the firedamp in, which would also burn. But it conducted the heat away so that the firedamp outside the lamp was not heated to its ignition temperature and so did not explode.

The Davy lamp was very successful. After its introduction the number of explosions in mines was greatly reduced. Even when battery operated lights were introduced to mines 100 years later, miners still used some Davy lamps to give them early warning of firedamp building up. The flame in the Davy lamp changes shape, becoming much longer, if there is any firedamp present.

Other interests

When Davy was President of the Royal Society he became one of the founders of the Zoological Society. He persuaded the new society to set up a Zoological Gardens in Regents Park. This Zoological Gardens is now London Zoo.

Looking at Cars and Air Pollution

LOOKING AT: BURNING AND BONDING

1 Write down any reasons you can think of why the cyclist in the picture is wearing a face mask.

What happens inside a car's engine?

The main part of the engine consists of hollow **cylinders** – four in most cars. Each cylinder has an inlet valve through which a mixture of petrol vapour and air is drawn in, and an outlet valve through which the waste exhaust gases are forced out. There is a spark plug in the cylinder which ignites the petrol–air mixture by an electrically produced spark. The exploding mixture pushes a piston down, which turns a shaft and makes the car move.

What happens during the explosion – the theory

Ideally, all the petrol burns with oxygen from the air and becomes carbon dioxide and water.

$$2C_8H_{18} + 25O_2 \rightarrow 16CO_2 + 18H_2O$$

Octane, one of the hydrocarbons in petrol

What happens in practice

- The petrol is not all burned so the exhaust gases contain some unburnt hydrocarbons. Hydrocarbons are greenhouse gases. Methane is 70 times more effective than carbon dioxide at stopping radiation leaving the Earth.
- Some of the carbon in the hydrocarbons is converted to carbon monoxide, rather than carbon dioxide.

$$2C_8H_{18} + 17O_2 \rightarrow 16CO + 18H_2O$$

Carbon monoxide is extremely poisonous. It is absorbed by haemoglobin in the blood and prevents the haemoglobin transporting oxygen around your body.

- Also, because the temperature in the engine is very high, some of the nitrogen in the air combines with some of the oxygen to form oxides of nitrogen such as nitrogen monoxide, NO, and nitrogen dioxide, NO_2. These gases contribute to acid rain.
- Some cars still use leaded petrol. The lead compound in this petrol helps their engines to work more efficiently. But the lead compounds produced in the exhaust gases are poisonous.

1 (a) Inlet valve opens
   (b) Piston moves down
   (c) Petrol–air mixture drawn into cylinder

2 (a) Both valves closed
   (b) Piston moves up, compressing the petrol–air mixture

3 (a) Spark plug ignites petrol–air mixture
   (b) Expanding hot gases push down piston

4 (a) Exhaust valve opens
   (b) Piston moves up, pushing exhaust gases out of cylinder

2 Sketch a car, or just draw a box to represent its engine, and add labelled arrows to summarize what substances go into the engine and what substances come out.

LOOKING AT: BURNING AND BONDING

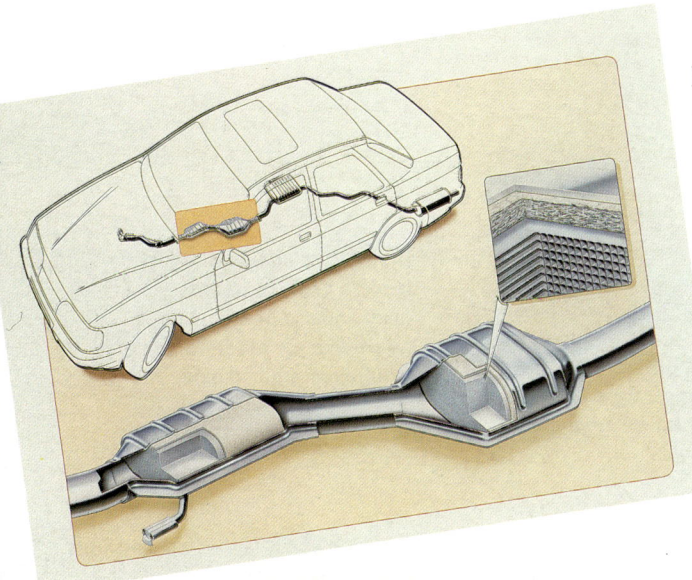

How can we reduce the pollution from cars?
Using unleaded petrol reduces the amount of lead in the environment. Many cars now run on unleaded petrol – their engines have been designed to work efficiently without lead.

One way of cutting down on the more powerful pollutants in exhaust gases is to use a **catalytic convertor**. This is a pipe containing a honeycomb structure coated with tiny particles of platinum. The platinum acts as a catalyst, speeding up reactions which:

- reduce the oxides of nitrogen
- oxidize unburnt hydrocarbons and carbon monoxide.

3 Why do you think catalytic convertors are expensive?
4 Why do you think convertors have a honeycombed internal structure?

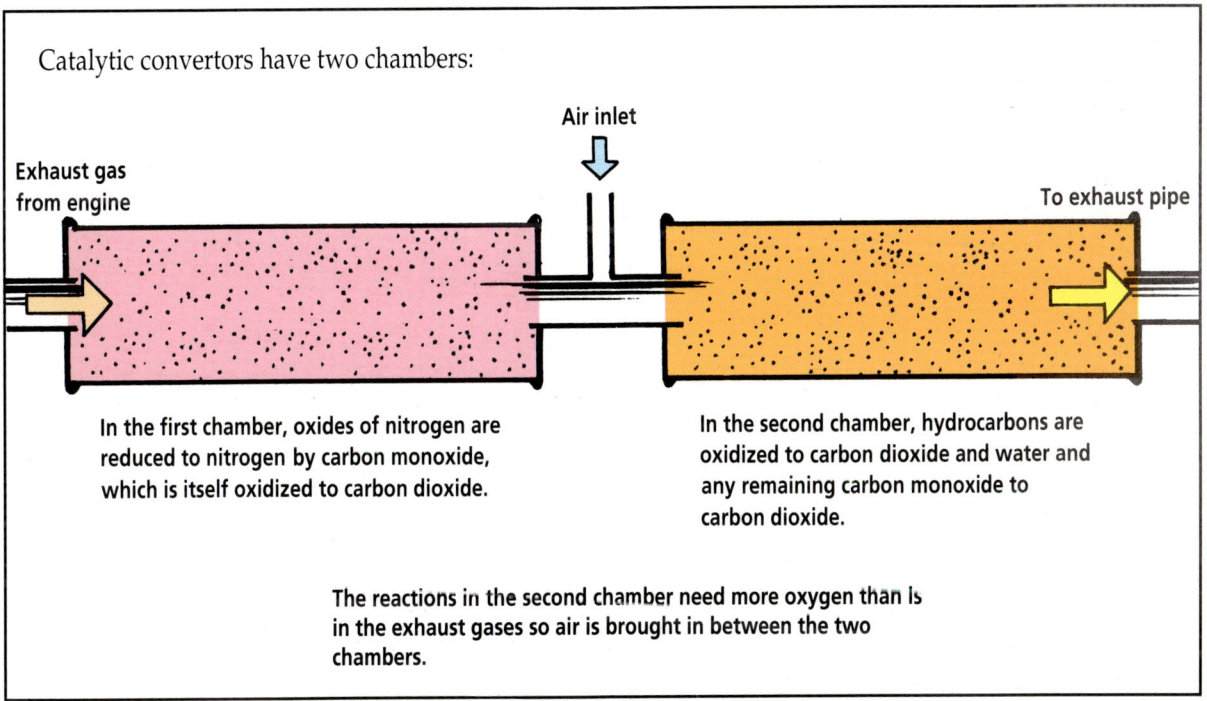

Catalytic convertors have two chambers:

Exhaust gas from engine → Air inlet → To exhaust pipe

In the first chamber, oxides of nitrogen are reduced to nitrogen by carbon monoxide, which is itself oxidized to carbon dioxide.

In the second chamber, hydrocarbons are oxidized to carbon dioxide and water and any remaining carbon monoxide to carbon dioxide.

The reactions in the second chamber need more oxygen than is in the exhaust gases so air is brought in between the two chambers.

The catalyst works best in the form of tiny particles which have a large surface area, rather than in big lumps. It will not work with leaded petrol. The catalyst absorbs the lead compounds on its surface and stops working. Lead poisons the catalyst.

5 Design a poster to persuade people to fit catalytic convertors to their cars.
6 Work out a balanced equation for the reaction in the first chamber between nitrogen oxide, NO, and carbon monoxide, CO.
7 Suggest a theory which would explain the action of the catalyst and the observations in the paragraph opposite.

In brief

Burning and bonding

1 Burning fuels

(a) Petrol and diesel fuel are mixtures of **hydrocarbons**. Natural gas (methane, CH_4) and bottled gas (propane, C_3H_8 or butane, C_4H_{10}) are also hydrocarbons.

(b) These fuels belong to a series of hydrocarbons called **alkanes**.

(c) When hydrocarbon fuels burn in a good supply of air, carbon dioxide and water are formed.

(d) The **flashpoint** of a fuel is the lowest temperature at which its vapour can be ignited.

(e) A certain amount of energy has to be transferred to the molecules before they will react. This is called the **activation energy**.

(f) During burning bonds are **broken** in the **reactants** (methane and oxygen) and new bonds are **made** to form the **products** (carbon dioxide and water).

(g) Breaking bonds in the reactants uses energy. Making new bonds in the products releases energy. More energy is released making the products than is used to break the bonds in the reactants. This means that overall the reaction is **exothermic**.

2 The effects of burning fuels on the atmosphere

The diagram shows the major effects on the atmosphere of burning fuels.

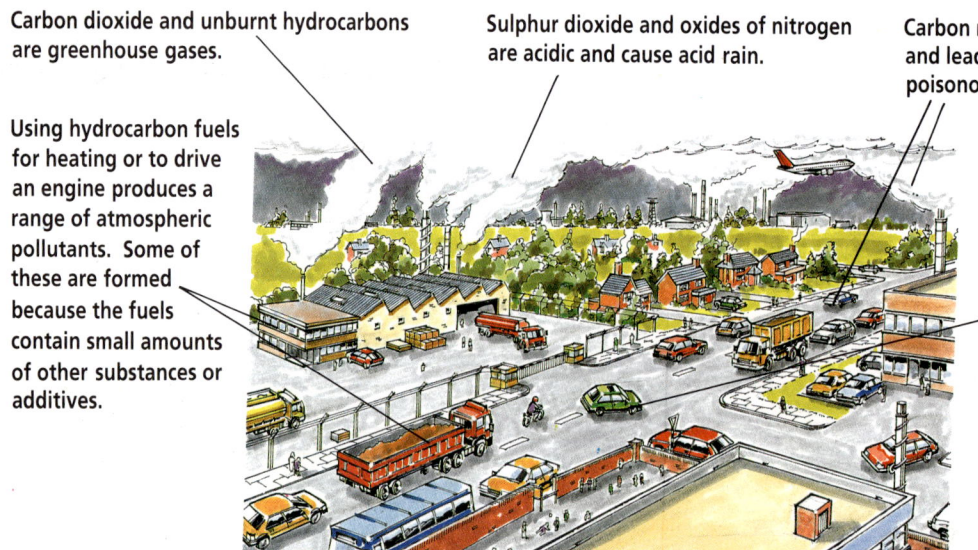

Carbon dioxide and unburnt hydrocarbons are greenhouse gases.

Using hydrocarbon fuels for heating or to drive an engine produces a range of atmospheric pollutants. Some of these are formed because the fuels contain small amounts of other substances or additives.

Sulphur dioxide and oxides of nitrogen are acidic and cause acid rain.

Carbon monoxide, oxides of nitrogen and lead compounds are particularly poisonous.

Catalytic convertors in exhaust systems convert carbon monoxide and hydrocarbons to carbon dioxide and water, and oxides of nitrogen to nitrogen.

IN BRIEF: BURNING AND BONDING 55

3 Theories of bonding and structure

Most minerals are compounds of metallic and non-metallic elements. Electrons are transferred from the metal atoms to the non-metal atoms forming positively and negatively charged **ions**. The attraction between these ions is called **ionic bonding**. It holds the particles in the crystals together.

Some compounds such as hydrocarbons are made from two or more non-metallic elements. Each bond between two atoms consists of a pair of shared electrons. The atoms in the molecules are held together by **covalent bonding**.

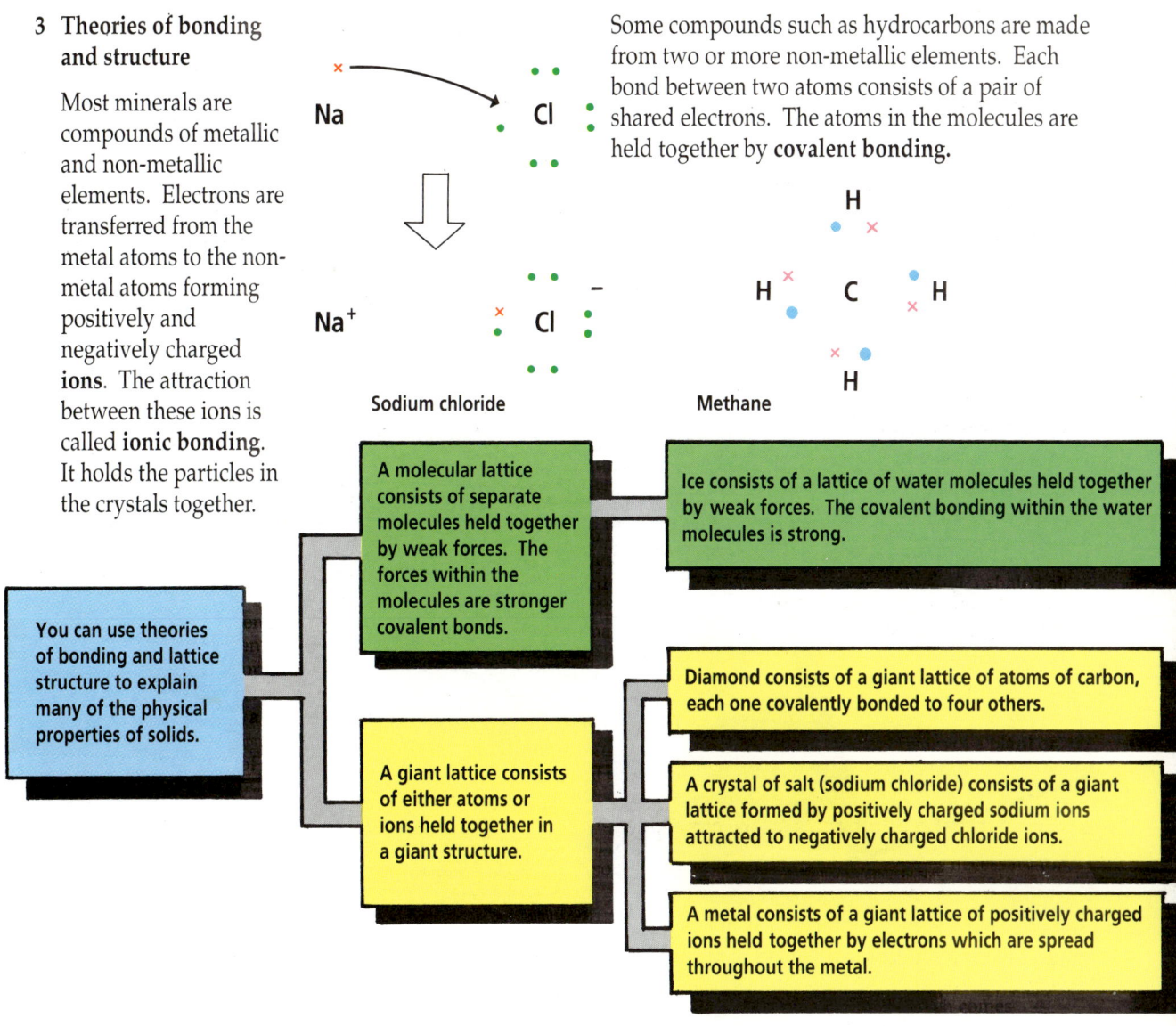

Sodium chloride

Methane

You can use theories of bonding and lattice structure to explain many of the physical properties of solids.

A molecular lattice consists of separate molecules held together by weak forces. The forces within the molecules are stronger covalent bonds.

Ice consists of a lattice of water molecules held together by weak forces. The covalent bonding within the water molecules is strong.

A giant lattice consists of either atoms or ions held together in a giant structure.

Diamond consists of a giant lattice of atoms of carbon, each one covalently bonded to four others.

A crystal of salt (sodium chloride) consists of a giant lattice formed by positively charged sodium ions attracted to negatively charged chloride ions.

A metal consists of a giant lattice of positively charged ions held together by electrons which are spread throughout the metal.

4 How the periodic table links properties of elements and their electronic structures

Li 2,1	The vertical columns of elements in the periodic table are called groups. Elements within the same group have similar properties. There is often a gradual variation in properties as you go up or down a group.	Elements in the same group have similar properties because they have the same number of outer electrons. You can link the trends in properties within a group to the changes in the size of the atoms as you go up or down the group.	F 2,7	Ne 2,8
Na 2,8,1			Cl 2,8,7	Ar 2,8,8
K 2,8,8,1			Br 2,8,18,7	Kr 2,8,18,8

Thinking about
Burning and Bonding

1. What happens when a hydrocarbon fuel burns?

The simplest hydrocarbon fuel is methane, CH_4. The 'natural gas' which many people use in their homes for cooking and heating is mainly methane. To help understand what happens when methane burns, first look at the evidence that is available.

Energy in the form of heat and light is given out when the fuel burns. You can feel the heat and you can see the light. A flame shows energy being released in the form of light.

You need to heat some of the fuel to start it burning. You can use a lighted match.

You know that when a hydrocarbon burns, it combines with oxygen. If there is a good supply of oxygen, the products are carbon dioxide and water.

You can interpret these observations in a number of ways which gradually give you a more detailed picture of what happens.

Word equation
methane + oxygen → carbon dioxide + water + energy (heat and light)
            started by
            heating

Chemical equation
$$CH_4 + 2O_2 \rightarrow CO_2 + 2H_2O + \text{energy (heat and light)}$$

This shows that a molecule of

- methane contains one carbon atom and four hydrogen atoms
- oxygen contains two oxygen atoms
- carbon dioxide contains one carbon atom and two oxygen atoms
- water contains two hydrogen atoms and one oxygen atom.

The equation also shows that for every methane molecule burned, two oxygen molecules are used, and one carbon dioxide and two water molecules are formed.

Bond breaking and bond making

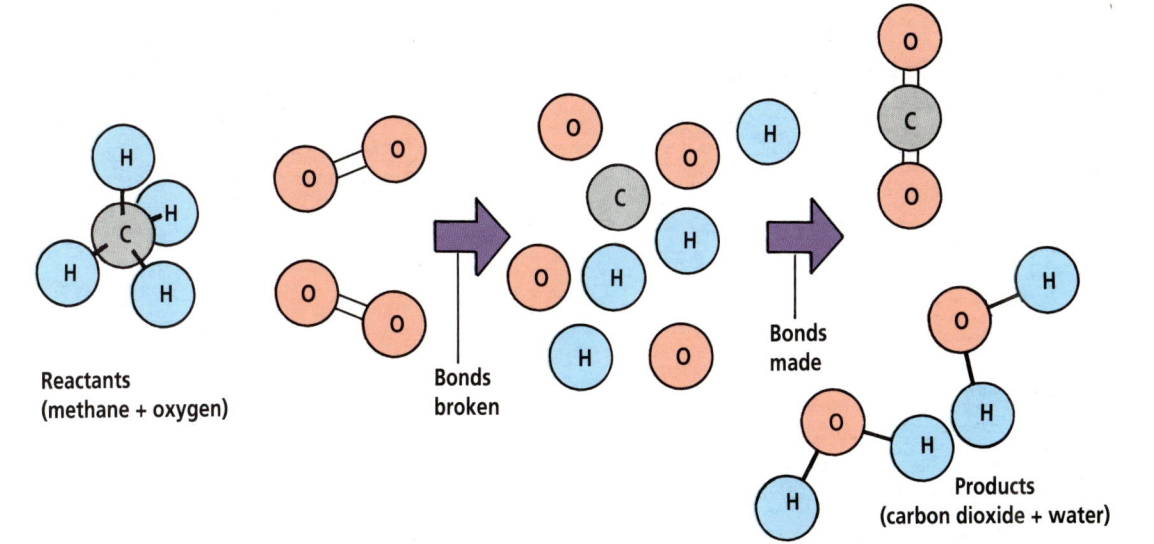

Energy changes

Energy is needed to break the bonds in the reactants because you are pulling apart atoms that want to stay together.

Energy is given out when new bonds are made in the products because the atoms want to stick together.

The energy given out is greater than the energy needed, so the reaction is **exothermic** (gives out energy as heat). An energy level diagram shows this. (Burning also gives out energy as light.)

Although the reaction gives out energy as heat and light, it does not happen spontaneously. You have to ignite the methane and oxygen to start them burning. You have to provide energy to start the reaction. This energy is called the **activation energy**.

You can see this on the second energy level diagram.

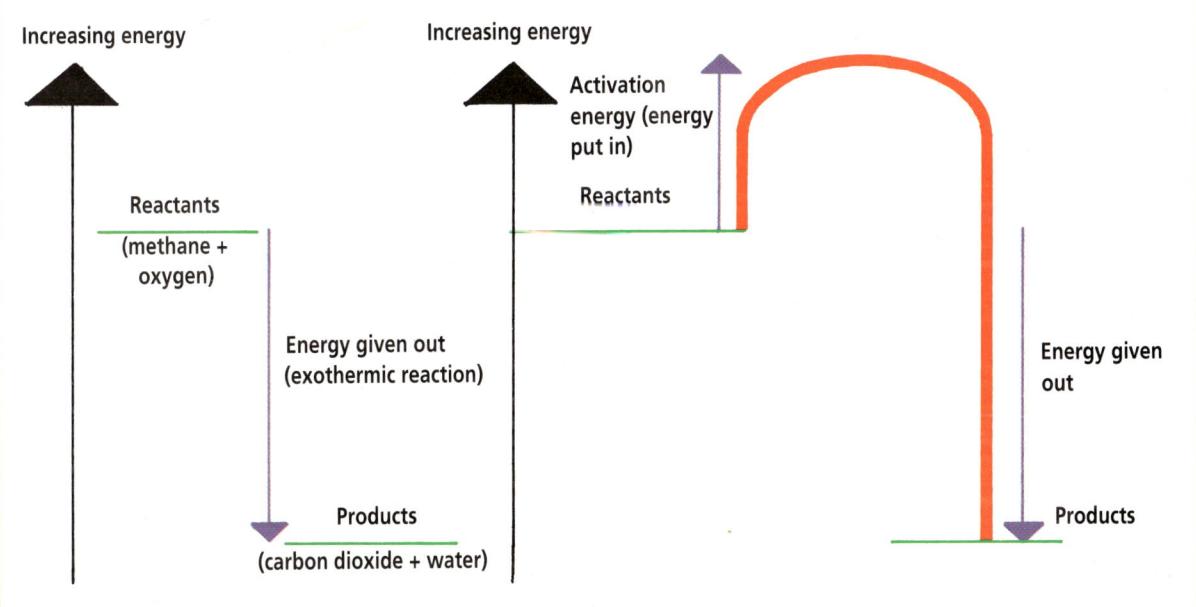

2. How do atoms in compounds stick together?

Salt (sodium chloride) is a compound made from the elements sodium and chlorine.

Sodium is a soft metal which reacts violently with water.

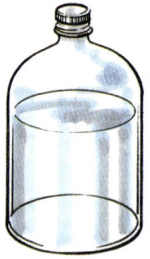
Carbon tetrachloride (tetrachloromethane) is a colourless liquid which was used for cleaning marks off clothes until it was found to have a harmful vapour. It is a compound of carbon and chlorine.

Carbon is a black solid.

Chlorine is a poisonous green gas.

The observations in the diagram need a lot of explaining! What happens to the sodium and chlorine atoms when they combine to form salt? What happens to the carbon and chlorine atoms when they combine to form carbon tetrachloride?

Although both salt and carbon tetrachloride contain chlorine, they have very different properties.

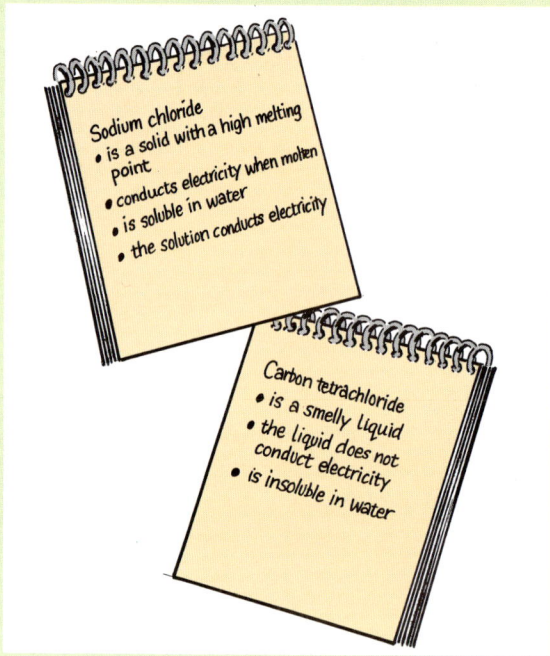

Sodium chloride
- is a solid with a high melting point
- conducts electricity when molten
- is soluble in water
- the solution conducts electricity

Carbon tetrachloride
- is a smelly liquid
- the liquid does not conduct electricity
- is insoluble in water

Any theories about how the elements in these compounds are bonded together need to explain these different properties.

A theory to explain the properties of salt
If you investigate what happens when molten salt conducts electricity, you find that the sodium parts of the compound move to the negative electrode and the chloride parts to the positive.

Sodium chloride consists of positively and negatively charged particles called **ions**.

An ion is formed when an atom loses or gains a certain number of electrons. It does this to achieve a stable electron arrangement. See *Thinking About 4* on page 62 for more details of this. For some atoms it is easier to achieve this by losing electrons. For others it is easier to gain electrons.

Sodium and chloride ions are formed because one electron is transferred from each sodium atom to a chlorine atom. An electron has a charge of −1.

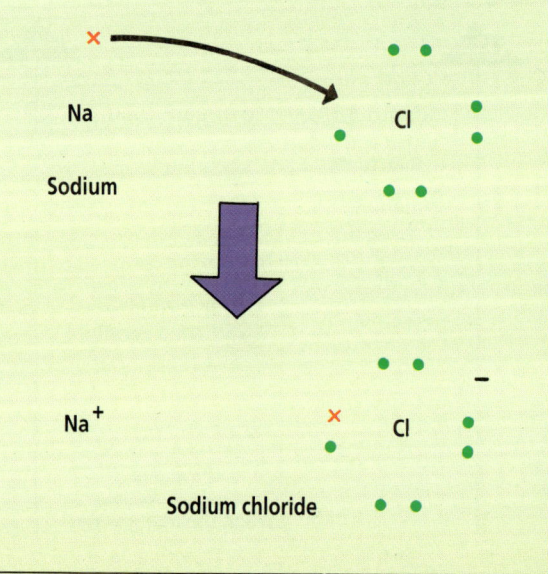

Because the sodium ion now has one less electron, it has an overall charge of +1. Because the chloride ion now has one extra electron, it has an overall charge of –1.

These oppositely charged ions attract each other. When millions and millions of them come together a crystal of salt is formed. This type of bonding is called **ionic bonding**.

When salt melts, the ions can move around. Because the forces between the ions are strong it takes a lot of energy to melt salt, so it has a high melting point.

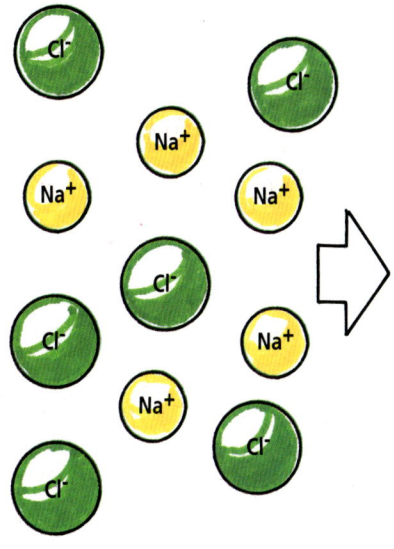

Oppositely charged ions come together to form...

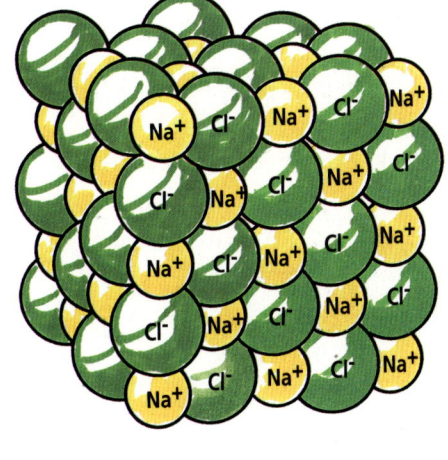

... a crystal structure

A theory to explain the properties of carbon tetrachloride

Carbon tetrachloride does not conduct electricity so it does not contain ions. How do the atoms stick together?

For carbon to form a stable electron arrangement (see *Thinking About 4*) it is easier to share electrons with chlorine rather than lose or gain them. It can share four additional electrons, one each from four chlorine atoms.

The electrons are negatively charged and the nuclei of the atoms are positively charged, so the shared pairs of electrons hold the atoms together rather like a piece of double-sided sellotape!

These bonds are called **covalent bonds**. Each atom can only form a certain number of covalent bonds.

Solid carbon tetrachloride melts at the low temperature of –23°C. When it melts the molecules remain intact. The forces between the molecules are relatively weak, so the molecules can move around easily, even at low temperatures.

How do these theories explain solubility in water?

Water molecules are unusual in that the hydrogen parts of the molecule are slightly positively charged and the oxygen part is slightly negatively charged. These small charges enable water molecules to pull sodium and chloride ions off the salt crystals and so salt will dissolve in water.

Because carbon tetrachloride molecules do not have any charges on them, water cannot pull them apart and so carbon tetrachloride is not soluble in water.

3. How does the periodic table explain the properties of elements?

You can observe properties of elements and compounds. You can then use theories of bonding to explain these properties. This is helpful, but there are over 90 elements which combine together to form thousands of different compounds. Because of this, early chemists looked for *patterns* in the behaviour of elements and compounds before they began to develop theories of bonding. The arrangement of the elements called the **periodic table** makes many of these patterns more obvious.

In 1869, Dimitri Mendeleev was the first chemist to develop an arrangement of the elements which resembled the modern periodic table.

The shape of the periodic table was worked out by
- **putting the elements in order.**
  Most elements are placed in order of increasing mass of their atoms. Hydrogen atoms have the smallest mass so hydrogen comes first. (*Thinking About 4* on page 62 explains that in fact the elements are placed in order of the number of protons in their atoms. This is roughly the same as the order of mass of the atoms. The early chemists who developed the periodic table did not know about protons.)

- **starting a new line** so that elements which are similar to each other end up in the same vertical column or **group**.

Looking at two of these groups shows how useful the periodic table is in making patterns of properties more obvious.

Group I

The elements in group I all look similar. They are soft metals, which are shiny when cut but rapidly tarnish in the air.

They are all reactive metals. If you add them to water they react vigorously giving off hydrogen gas and leaving an alkaline solution. For example:

sodium + water → sodium hydroxide + hydrogen

$2Na + 2H_2O \rightarrow 2NaOH + H_2$

This is why the group I metals are called the **alkali metals**.

Although the group I metals are all similar, there is a trend within the group. They become more reactive as you go down the group. Sodium is more reactive than lithium, potassium is more reactive than sodium, and so on.

Group I	Group II						
Li 3	Be 4						
Na 11	Mg 12						
K 19	Ca 20	Sc 21	Ti 22	V 23	Cr 24	Mn 25	Fe 26
Rb 37	Sr 38	Y 39	Zr 40	Nb 41	Mo 42	Tc 43	Ru 44
Cs 55	Ba 56	La 57	Hf 72	Ta 73	W 74	Re 75	Os 76
Fr 87	Ra 88	Ac 89					

H
I

Group VII

The elements in group VII are reactive non-metals. For example, they will all react with sodium metal to form similar compounds:

fluorine + sodium → sodium flouride
F_2 + 2Na → 2NaF

chlorine + sodium → sodium chloride
Cl_2 + 2Na → 2NaCl

bromine + sodium → sodium bromide
Br_2 + 2Na → 2NaBr

iodine + sodium → sodium iodide
I_2 + 2Na → 2NaI

These sodium compounds are all white crystalline solids which have high melting points and are soluble in water. They are salts.

The group VII elements are called the **halogens** after the Greek for salt producing (*hals gen*).

Unlike the alkali metals, the halogens become *less* reactive as you go down the group. That is, fluorine is more reactive than chlorine, which is more reactive than bromine, and so on.

It is easy to show this by adding chlorine water to sodium bromide solution – you can see bromine being formed. Similarly, if you add chlorine water to sodium iodide solution, you can see iodine being formed:

These are called **displacement reactions**. The more reactive halogen displaces the less reactive halogen from its compound. You should be able to predict what would happen if you added bromine to sodium iodide solution.

Bromine is more rare than chlorine. Sea water contains sodium bromide (as well as sodium chloride). It is economically worthwhile extracting bromine from sea water by passing chlorine into it. The chlorine displaces the bromine.

$$Cl_2 + 2NaBr \rightarrow 2NaCl + Br_2$$

This works on Anglesey extracts bromine from sea water.

4. How can we explain the patterns in the periodic table?

Looking at the electronic structures of atoms provides explanations for some of the patterns in the periodic table.

How many protons?
The order of the elements in the periodic table is based on the number of protons in the nucleus of an atom of each element.
- The first element, hydrogen, has one proton
- the second, helium, has 2 protons
- the 20th element, calcium, has 20 protons, and so on.

This number is called the **atomic number** of the element.

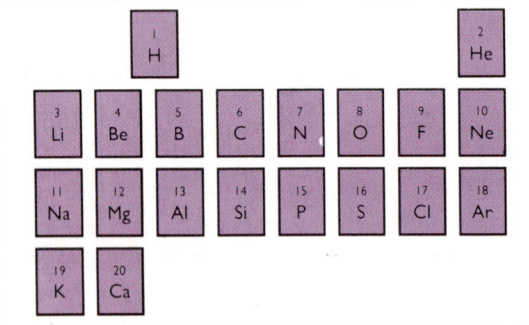

The numbers of protons in the atoms of the first 20 elements

From the evidence available we believe that half a proton cannot exist. This means that another element between, say, potassium and calcium, cannot exist anywhere in the universe.

How many electrons?
Each proton has a single positive charge so, for example, the nucleus of a carbon atom has a charge of +6. Atoms have no overall charge so the atomic number tells us how many electrons are in an atom of that element. The number of negatively charged electrons must exactly balance the number of protons.

This means that if you know the atomic number of an element, you can work out how many protons are in the nucleus of an atom of the element, and how many electrons there are around the nucleus.

How are the electrons arranged?
The electrons around the nucleus of an atom are grouped so that electrons with similar energies are placed together. Each group is called a **shell**.

For the first 18 elements there are three shells. The first contains electrons with the lowest energy. It can hold up to 2 electrons. The second and third shells can each hold up to 8 electrons. So you can work out electron arrangements from atomic numbers. The most stable elements are the noble gases which all have full outer shells.

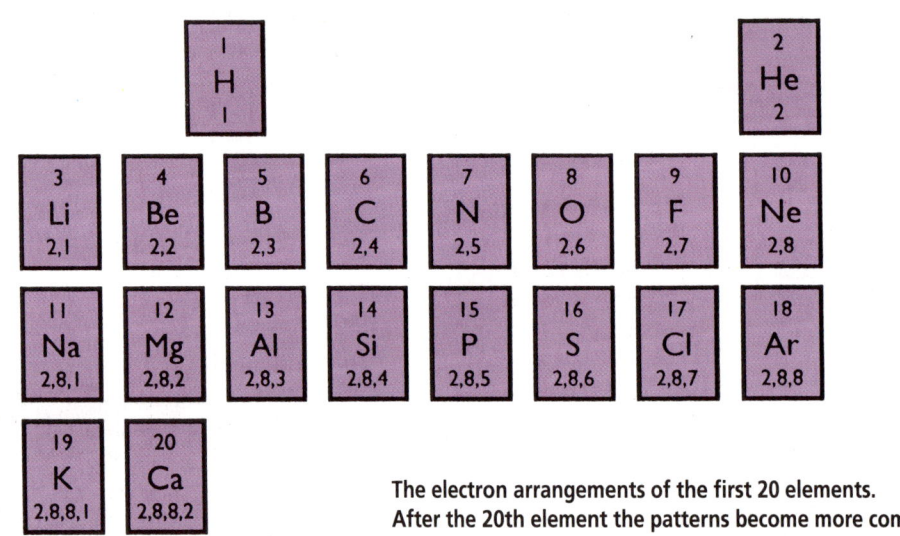

The electron arrangements of the first 20 elements.
After the 20th element the patterns become more complicated.

Now look at the outer electron arrangements of the elements in each group. You will see that they are identical. Group I elements have one outer electron and group VII elements have seven outer electrons. This is why elements in the same group have similar properties.

Ionic bonding
The outer electron of group I elements, such as sodium, can be transferred to an atom of another element, such as chlorine. So group I elements all form ions with a charge of +1. In each case the ion formed has a full outer shell of electrons – a stable arrangement. A group I metal only has to lose one electron to achieve this arrangement. All group II metals have two electrons in their outer shell. So, in order to achieve a full outer shell they lose two electrons and form, for example, Ca^{2+} ions.

All the group VII elements can accept an electron in their outer shell and so form ions with a charge of –1.

Covalent bonding
For an element such as carbon, which has four electrons in its outer shell, or nitrogen which has five outer electrons, it is easier to achieve a full outer shell by sharing electrons with other atoms. Bonds formed by sharing electrons are **covalent bonds**. Ammonia, NH_3, is one compound which has covalent bonds.

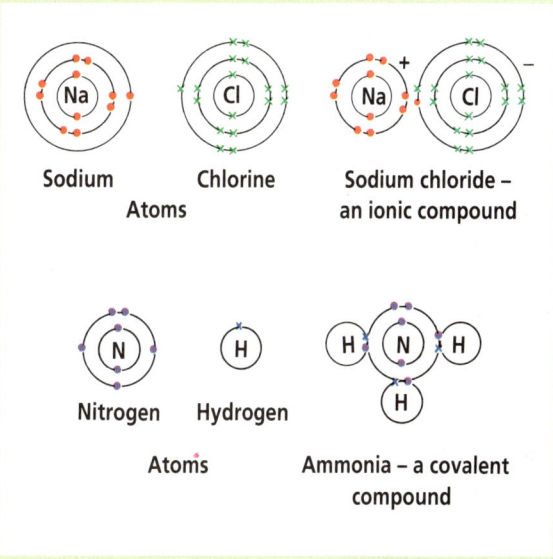

There are elements such as chlorine (seven outer electrons) which achieve a full outer shell by gaining electrons to form ions when they react with some elements, and by sharing electrons when they react with others.

How do we explain trends down a group?
Although all the group I metals react in the same way, they become more reactive as you go down the group.

They all react by losing their outer electron. Electrons are held in the atom by the positively charged nucleus. So an outer electron will be more easily removed from a large atom than from a small atom because it is further away from the nucleus. This explains why sodium is more reactive than lithium.

The halogens become more reactive as you go up the group. They all react by gaining an electron in their outer shell. This electron will be more readily gained by a small atom than a large atom because the electron will be closer to the nucleus of the atom and so held more strongly. This explains why fluorine is more reactive than chlorine.

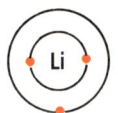

The outer electron is held by the positive nucleus. There are only two electrons shielding the outer electron from the nucleus.

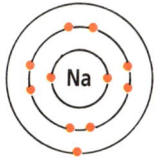

The outer electron is further from the positive nucleus and is shielded by the ten inner electrons. Sodium loses its outer electron more readily than lithium so is more reactive.

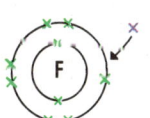

An extra outer electron approaching the atom is close to the positive nucleus.

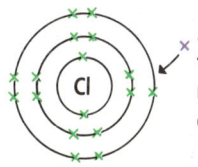

An extra outer electron approaching the atom is further from the positive nucleus and is shielded by the inner electrons. Chlorine gains an electron less easily than fluorine so is less reactive.

5. How do atoms in elements stick together?

Thinking About 2 on pages 58–9 discussed how we can explain the properties of compounds formed from two elements using theories of ionic and covalent bonding. In a solid element there is only one type of atom, so how are the atoms bonded together? Again we can look for clues in the properties of the solids.

Metals

One property that all metals have in common is that they conduct electricity. This means that there are some charged particles in metals which can move. These charged particles are electrons.

When a piece of a metal conducts electricity, the outer electrons of the atoms are moving through the metal. A metal atom without its outer electrons becomes a positively charged ion.

You can think of a metal as a giant structure of positively charged metal ions with negatively charged electrons spread between the ions, holding them together.

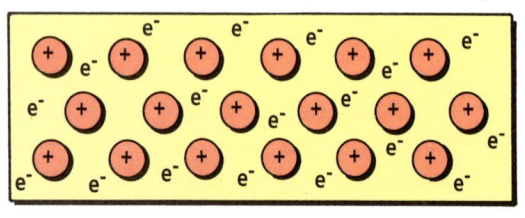

You can see crystals on the surface of this zinc. They are formed by the zinc ions packing together in a particular pattern as the metal changes from liquid to solid.

Carbon

One form of carbon is diamond. It is very hard and melts at the high temperature of 3550°C. It does not conduct electricity. This suggests that the atoms are held together very strongly and there are no charged particles which are free to move.

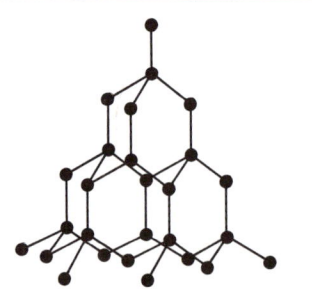

Diamond is a giant structure in which the carbon atoms are held together by covalent bonds.

Each carbon atom has four outer electrons and can form four covalent bonds with four other carbon atoms. Each of these atoms also forms four bonds with other atoms, and so on. A diamond is millions and millions of atoms bonded together in this way. It is a very strong structure with a very high melting point.

The other form of carbon is graphite. Graphite is soft and slippery. This suggests that parts of the structure are not held strongly to each other, so they can slide past each other. Graphite conducts electricity so there must be some charged particles which are able to move.

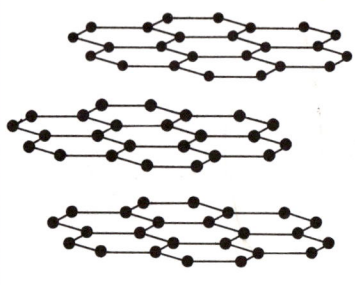

Graphite consists of layers of carbon atoms.

Each carbon atom within a layer is held to three other carbon atoms by covalent bonds. This means that each carbon is using only three of its four outer electrons for these bonds. The fourth electron is able to move. This is why graphite, even though it is a non-metal, will conduct electricity.

The layers of carbon atoms have only weak bonds between them. They will move over each other. This is why graphite is slippery.

Things to do

Burning and Bonding

Things to try out

1 Sugar and salt are both white crystalline substances which dissolve in water. But only the salt solution will conduct electricity. Using a torch, a torch battery and some pieces of wire, demonstrate this to a member of your family or a friend. Then explain to them why there is this difference between sugar and salt.

Things to find out

2 Look at the periodic table on pages 60–61. The row of elements between scandium, Sc, and zinc, Zn, is called the **transition elements**. Look at these elements and see which of them you have heard of. Make a table of these comparing their properties and uses. Use reference books to help you.

Things to write about

3 An analysis of a piece of rock from the Moon shows that it contains the elements calcium, aluminium, silicon and oxygen. These elements are also found in rocks on Earth. Write an article aimed at 16-year-olds which reports this fact and explains why we could not expect to find any elements on the Moon which cannot also be found on Earth.

Points to discuss

4 Continue this conversation so that it includes an explanation of what happens when the paper is burnt. Do you think it is better to burn the paper, let it rot away or recycle it?

5 Some people are against using catalytic convertors in motor cars because they result in more carbon dioxide being formed. Carbon dioxide is a greenhouse gas. Discuss the validity of this argument. Do you think catalytic convertors should be used?

6 Discuss what the differences are between atoms, molecules and ions. Try to agree on a pictorial way of describing how they are related to each other.

Questions to answer

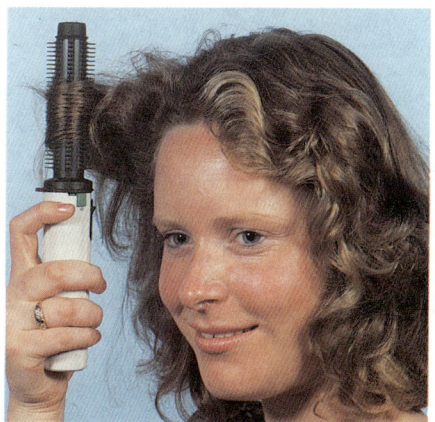

7 The hair curler uses butane, C_4H_{10}, as a fuel. The butane is stored under pressure as a liquid. When the curler is switched on, butane is released and changes to a gas. The gas is ignited by a spark.

(a) Describe the arrangement of the molecules of butane when it is a liquid and when it is a gas. Suggest why it is a liquid when under pressure and why it changes to a gas when it is released.

(b) At normal atmospheric pressure butane boils at 0°C. Explain why it has such a low boiling point.

(c) Using lines for bonds, draw a molecule of butane. What type of bonds hold the atoms together? Using dots and crosses for electrons, explain how these bonds are formed.

(d) Draw an energy level diagram to show the energy changes which occur when butane burns. Explain why a spark is needed to start the butane burning.

8 A group of students was asked to investigate a white crystalline solid. They found that it had the following properties:
- soluble in water
- insoluble in hexane
- the solution in water was a good conductor of electricity
- it could not be melted with a bunsen burner.

(a) Explain how this evidence provides clues about the type of bonding in the solid.

(b) Their teacher then told them that it contained a metal M with atomic number 20 and a non-metal X with atomic number 17. Draw the electronic structures of these two elements and then explain how the elements are bonded together in the solid.

(c) Explain what you would expect to happen if the students could have heated the solid to a sufficiently high temperature to melt it, and then passed a direct electric current through it.

9 Graphite is a solid which conducts electricity and is used in pencils.

Polythene is a solid which is easily softened by heating and moulded into different shapes. It does not conduct electricity.

Copper is a solid which can be drawn out into wires which are flexible but strong and which will conduct electricity.

Use theories of bonding and structure to explain the differences between these solids and how their uses depend of their properties. Write your explanation in a form which you think would be helpful to a 16-year-old science student. Use diagrams if you think they will help.

10 In the periodic table below some elements are identified by their symbols. Others are indicated by the letters **a** to **g**.

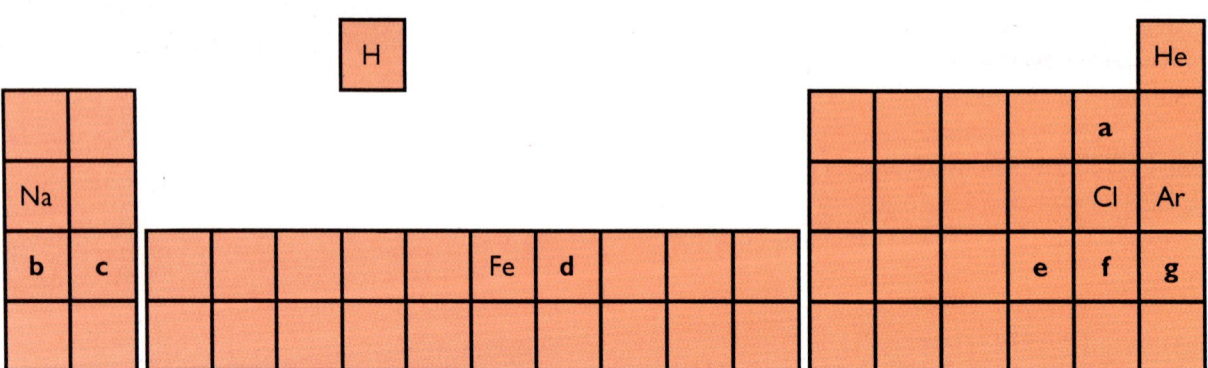

(a) From the elements **a** to **g** select the one which is likely to be
- a magnetic metal
- a soft solid which is shiny when freshly cut and which reacts violently with water
- a reactive gas
- an unreactive gas.

(b) Predict the formula of compounds formed by each of the following pairs of elements combining together. In each case, using dots and crosses to represent electrons, explain how you have made your predictions.
- **b** with **f**
- **c** with **a**
- **c** with **e**
- **H** with **f**
- **H** with **e**.

(c) Suggest why **b** is more reactive than sodium and why **a** is more reactive than chlorine.

Introducing

ENERGY TODAY AND TOMORROW

ENERGY TODAY AND TOMORROW

Every day we use energy in many different ways. The photos show a few examples.

Most of our energy in Britain comes from concentrated energy sources – the **fossil fuels** coal, gas and oil, and a small amount from the **nuclear fuel** uranium.

1. What fuel is being used in each photo?
2. One fuel is a *secondary* fuel. It has to be made from other (*primary*) fuels. Which one is this?
3. How might the jobs shown in the photos have been done 200 years ago? What fuels would have been used then?

Our lifestyle today is very different from that of people 200 years ago. Many of the things we take for granted in our modern way of living depend on fossil fuels. But the Earth's reserves of coal, oil and gas are limited. They will not last forever. If we go on using them at the present rate, gas and oil will probably run out in your lifetime. Coal and uranium will last a few hundred years more, but then they will also be used up.

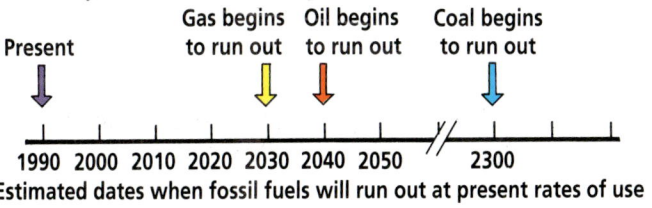

Estimated dates when fossil fuels will run out at present rates of use

In the future, will some historian draw a graph like this to show how we used up the Earth's store of concentrated fuels?

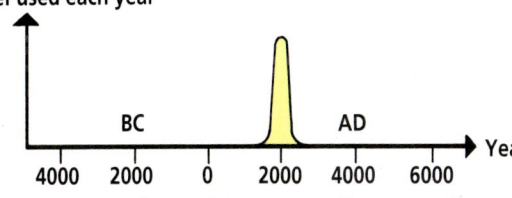

If so, perhaps our future historian will use much less energy than we do today. Her energy needs may be supplied by **renewable energy sources**: sun, wind and waves. Or perhaps scientists will by then have discovered how to tame nuclear fusion to provide unlimited energy for all.

IN THIS CHAPTER YOU WILL FIND OUT
- about the fuels we use and what we use them for
- how electricity is generated
- how different kinds of power station work and how electricity is distributed
- about renewable energy sources and how they could be used in the future.

Looking at Energy Self-sufficiency

LOOKING AT:
ENERGY TODAY AND TOMORROW

Getting away from it all

The Cook family have had enough of city life. They want to live somewhere more remote and unspoilt. They have just moved to a small house (with a kitchen, a living room and two bedrooms) on an island off the North of Scotland.

There is plenty of peat on the island which can be cut in the summer and stacked and dried to use as fuel. The stove in the kitchen can burn peat to heat the water. It also has hotplates and an oven for cooking. There is a fireplace in the living room.

There is no mains electricity on the island. This is a problem because Brian Cook earns his living by writing and uses a wordprocessor for about 3 hours every day. How can the Cook family generate enough electricity for their needs?

> 1 Make a list of all the things you and your family use electricity for. Divide these into two groups: those which can only be done by using electricity, and those for which another fuel could be used.

Making your own electricity

If you wanted to generate your own electricity, here are some of the things you might use.

Wind generators come in a range of sizes. This 50 W generator will provide 50 W in a moderate wind. If the wind drops, so does the output.

Solar cells are long lasting and reliable. An array about 1 m by 0.3 m will give a 40 W output in bright sunshine. If it is overcast, the output falls to less than 10 W.

You often want electricity when there is no wind or sunshine. So you need to **store** electricity. Connecting a generator to the terminals of a *rechargeable battery* causes chemical reactions inside the battery. You can later connect the charged battery into a circuit and the reverse reactions happen, producing electricity.

A 12 V tractor battery like this has a storage capacity of 90 ampere-hours. This means that each battery can store 90×12 watt-hours (=1080 Wh) of electrical energy. (Remember: power = current $\times$ voltage, $P = IV$). 1 Wh means 1 W of electrical power for 1 hour. Several batteries can be connected in parallel to provide more storage capacity. Battery storage is about 80% efficient; you get back about 80% of the electrical energy you put in.

LOOKING AT: ENERGY TODAY AND TOMORROW

A *regulator* is needed to stop the batteries being overcharged. Once the batteries are fully charged, any extra electricity generated is simply used to produce heat. Meters allow you to check that the system is working and to measure the amount of electricity in store.

Most electrical appliances are designed to run at mains voltage, 240 V a.c. The Cook family already own many of these. They will not work from 12 V d.c. batteries. An *inverter* is a device which takes a 12 V d.c. input and gives a 240 V a.c. output. This 250 W inverter provides a *total* power output of up to 250 W. Inverters are around 80% efficient.

Making choices

Here are some of the notes the Cooks made to help them reach a decision about their energy supply.

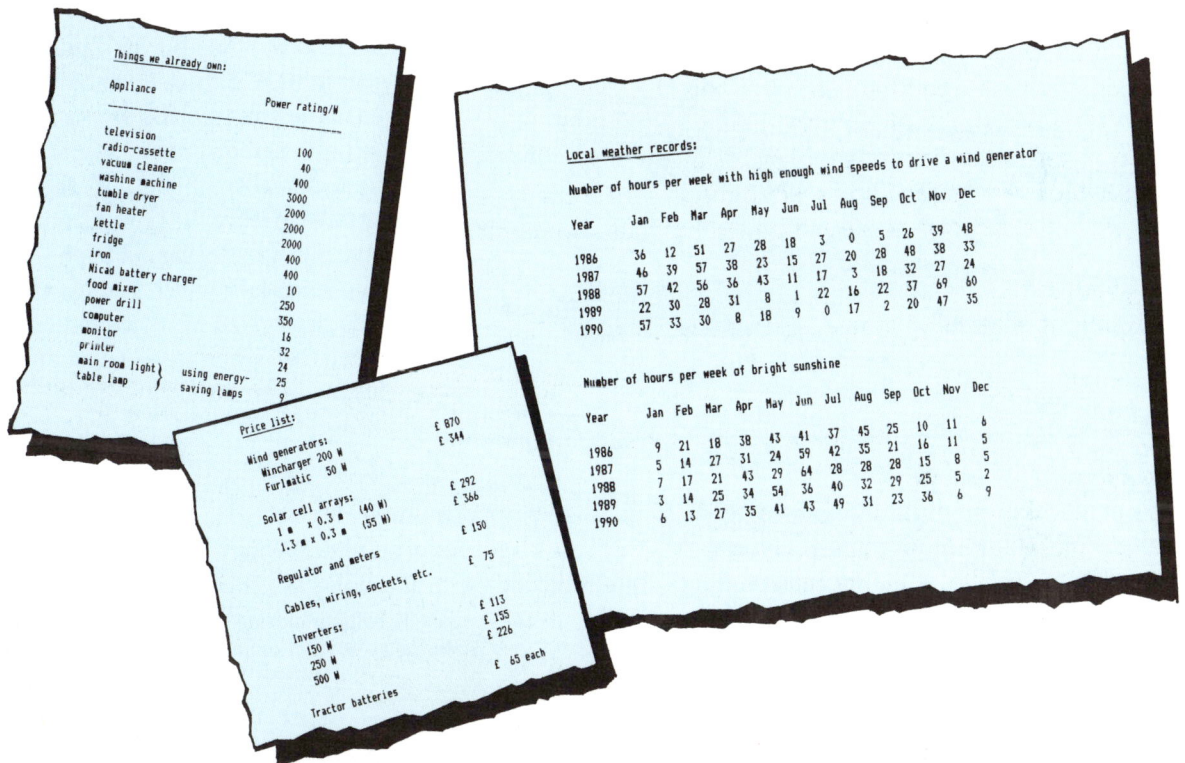

2 Would you advise the Cooks to use a solar panel or a wind generator as their main method of generating electricity? Or would you have both? Explain the reasons for your advice.

3 If you were moving to the island, which of the appliances in the list above would you plan to use? For each one that you choose, estimate the number of hours per week it will be used for. Use this to calculate the total number of watt-hours of electricity you will need to generate every week.

4 Use your result from question 3 to make an estimate of the amount of storage capacity you need. Explain your decision.

5 The Cooks have a budget of £1250 to spend on their electricity system. They may be able to add to it later. What do you think they should buy with this money? Explain the reasons for your decisions. You may need to go back and review your decisions in questions 3 and 4 to keep within your budget.

Looking at

Dealing with the Waste

LOOKING AT:
ENERGY TODAY AND TOMORROW

Energy flow...

You can think of a power station as a large energy converter. The input is the energy stored in the fuel and in the oxygen it combines with when it is burnt. The useful output is the electrical energy carried away from the power station to factories, offices and homes. The remainder of the energy output – about two-thirds of the total – is wasted.

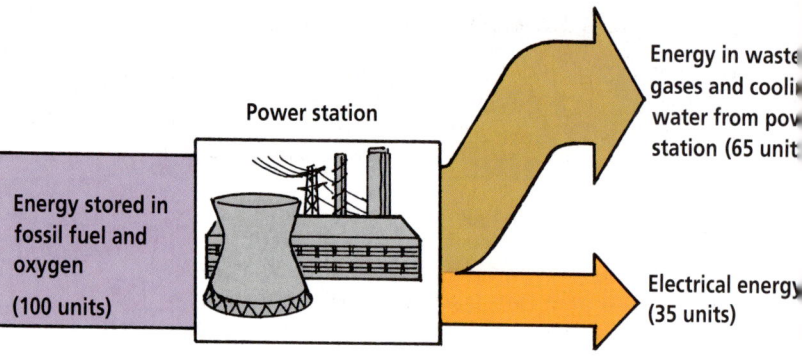

...and matter flow

As well as this energy flow, there is also a flow of matter through a power station. In a coal-fired power station, coal goes into the station. It reacts with oxygen in the furnace. The products of the reaction – carbon dioxide, water vapour and smaller amounts of other gases – have to leave the power station. Some parts of the coal cannot burn – these are left as ash, which also has to leave the power station. Electricity may be a 'clean fuel' when we use it, but it is not so clean to produce!

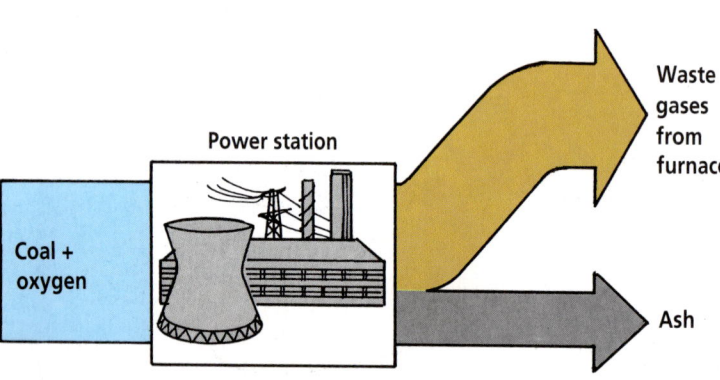

Acid rain

One of the waste products of coal-fired power stations is a particular problem. Coal contains a small amount of sulphur. In 100 tonnes of typical coal, there are 1.5 tonnes of sulphur. When the coal is burnt, the sulphur combines with oxygen to produce sulphur dioxide (SO_2), an acidic gas. The diagram shows what happens to this sulphur dioxide.

3 In sunlight, sulphur dioxide combines with more oxygen in the air to form sulphur trioxide (SO_3).

2 But most of it is carried high into the atmosphere in the plume of smoke from the power station chimney. It can then travel a very long distance from the power station.

4 Sulphur trioxide dissolves in water droplets, forming an acidic solution. When it rains, this falls to Earth as acidic rain.

1 Some sulphur dioxide comes back to the ground near the power station. This is called dry deposition.

5 Scientists think that acid rain from power stations in England may have made lakes in Scotland, Norway and Sweden more acidic. Some species of fish cannot survive in more acidic water. Acid rain also damages forests and corrodes the stonework of buildings.

Ways of reducing sulphur dioxide emissions
- Replace coal by a different fuel. Oil contains less sulphur than coal. Natural gas contains almost none.
- Use coal with less sulphur in it. This would have to come from abroad.
- Replace coal-fired power stations with nuclear ones or alternative energy sources, which do not emit sulphur dioxide.
- Remove the sulphur dioxide from the gases after burning the coal.

Cleaning up power stations
Britain, along with other European countries, has agreed to reduce sulphur dioxide pollution.

The electricity generating companies decided to switch to gas as the fuel for new power stations. But they have large coal-fired stations in operation. They plan to modify some of these to clean the gases after burning the coal. The method is called **flue-gas desulphurization** (**FGD**).

How does FGD work?
The diagram shows what happens in an FGD plant.

Sulphur dioxide is an acidic gas. Like all acids it is neutralized by alkalis. The alkali used in FGD is lime – calcium oxide (CaO). This is a very cheap alkali which is made from limestone.

The acidic sulphur dioxide reacts with the alkaline lime to form calcium sulphite ($CaSO_3$), which is a solid.

sulphur dioxide + calcium oxide (lime) → calcium sulphite

$SO_2(g) + CaO(s) \rightarrow CaSO_3(s)$

The calcium sulphite then reacts with oxygen in the air to form calcium sulphate ($CaSO_4$). Another name for this is **gypsum**.

calcium sulphite + oxygen → calcium sulphate

$2CaSO_3(s) + O_2(g) \rightarrow 2CaSO_4(s)$

Calcium sulphate is a useful chemical. It is used to make plaster, which is used in the building trade.

Too much of a good thing
FGD helps to tackle one environmental problem, but it also causes another. When the FGD plant at Drax power station in North Yorkshire is working, two train loads of limestone will arrive every day and three train loads of gypsum will need to be taken away. If all Britain's coal-fired power stations were fitted with FGD, they would produce 8 million tonnes of gypsum a year. The building industry uses about 3 million tonnes a year.

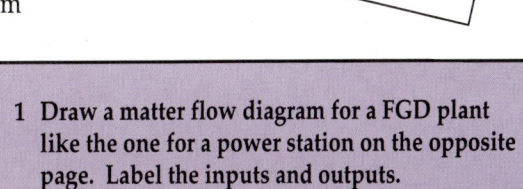

1. Draw a matter flow diagram for a FGD plant like the one for a power station on the opposite page. Label the inputs and outputs.
2. What would be the advantages and disadvantages of installing FGD at a power station:
   - for a person living near the power station
   - for a householder who has to pay electricity bills
   - for a person living several hundred miles downwind of the power station?
3. An electricity generating company plans to install FGD plants at its coal-fired power stations. But an FGD plant is expensive and not all power stations can be fitted at once. The company must decide which power station to fit with FGD first. What features of a power station would make it a good first choice?

Looking at

The National Grid

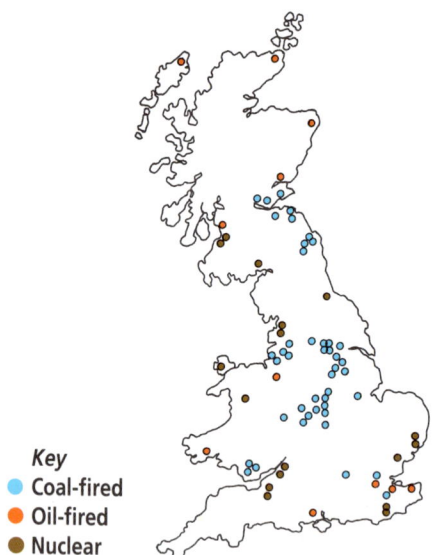

This map shows the main coal-fired, oil-fired and nuclear power stations in Britain.

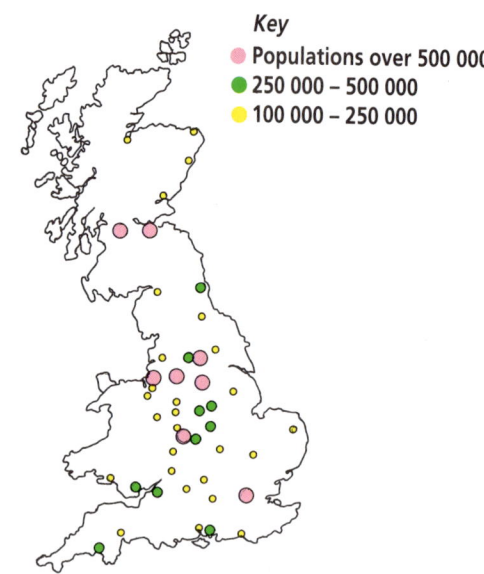

This map shows the areas of Britain where most people live.

1. Suggest some reasons why these sites have been chosen for coal-fired stations, oil-fired stations and nuclear power stations.
2. Why are power stations not situated near the largest cities, where most people live?

Getting electricity to the user

It is easier to move electricity around the country than to move fuels to power stations. All the power stations in Britain are connected into a massive network of cables and wires called the **National Grid**. All the users of electricity are also connected to the grid. This has several advantages:

- If users were just supplied by their 'local' power station, then their supply would be cut off every time the station needed repair or maintenance. With a grid system, when any station is shut down for repair, the others continue to supply electricity to the users.
- The amount of electricity needed varies during the day and during the year. The grid system allows us to use the most efficient stations almost all the time, with the older, less efficient ones coming on only at peak periods.

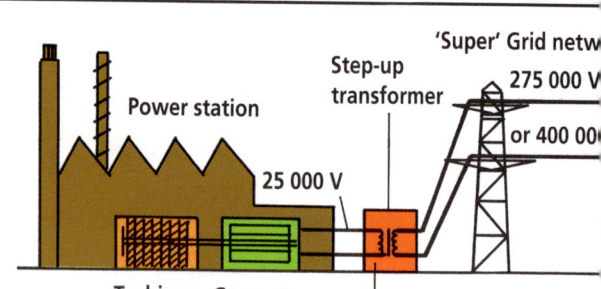

1. A power station generator can produce up to 8000 A at 25 000 V. Transformers at the power station step up the voltage and step down the current. Lower current means that thinner cables can be used and makes energy losses smaller. (This is explained in *Thinking About 7* on pages 85–6.)

LOOKING AT: ENERGY TODAY AND TOMORROW

5 A local transformer steps the voltage down from 11 000 V to 240 V for use in houses.

6 The wires from the local transformer station enter the meter and fuse box in your home – connecting you by wires and magnetic fields (in transformers) all the way back to the power station.

4 Large transformer substations step down the grid voltage to lower voltages for local use.

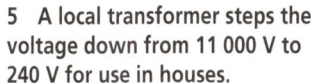

Step-down transformer | Grid network 132 000 V | 33 000 V | Heavy industry | Light industry | Offices | Homes

33 000 V   11 000 V   240 V

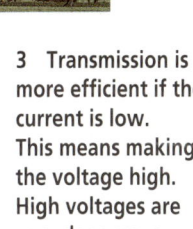

2 Pylon lines carry the cables from power stations all over the country.

3 Transmission is more efficient if the current is low. This means making the voltage high. High voltages are very dangerous.

3 Make a map of your local area. Mark on it any local transformer substations like the one in the photo above. Also mark any pylon lines and any large transformer substations. Draw lines to show how these must be connected (you cannot actually see the cables because some run underground).

4 Using the ideas explained in *Thinking About 7*, work out the turns ratio of
   (a) the transformers at a power station
   (b) substation transformers (both types)
   (c) a local transformer.

In brief

Energy Today and Tomorrow

1 Our way of life depends on using **fuels**. **Fossil fuels** (coal, oil and natural gas) and **nuclear fuels** (uranium and plutonium) provide a concentrated source of energy.

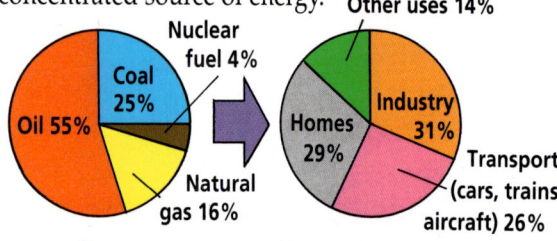

Sources of our energy — How we use energy

2 The Earth's reserves of fossil fuels and nuclear fuels are limited. They will not last forever. So it is important to conserve fossil fuels, by

- using fuels efficiently and avoiding waste
- developing alternative sources of energy, especially renewable sources.

3 When a fuel is used, its energy spreads out and becomes **dispersed**.

4 An electric current is generated when a wire moves through a magnetic field. This is called **electromagnetic induction**. The induced current is a **direct current**. If the wire moves in the opposite direction, the direction of the current changes.

5 A coil rotating in a magnetic field generates an **alternating** electric current.

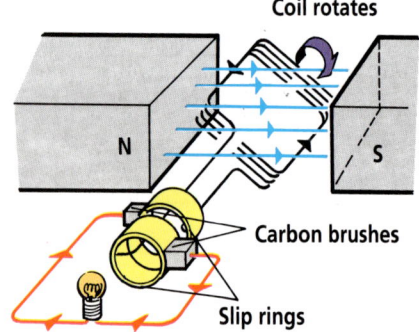

The current can be made bigger by
- using a stronger magnetic field
- rotating the coil faster
- using a coil with more turns
- winding the coil on a soft-iron core.

6 Most power stations use the energy in a fossil fuel or a nuclear fuel to boil water and make steam. This turns turbines which rotate a generator coil to produce electricity. About one-third of the energy stored in the fuel is turned into useful electricity; the rest is wasted in the hot flue gases and hot cooling water.

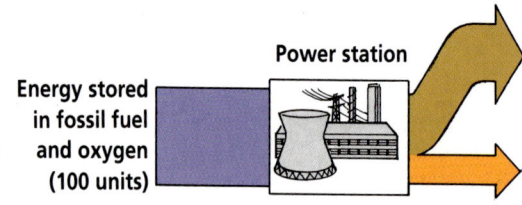

7 When a fossil fuel burns, it combines with oxygen in the air. This is a chemical process called **combustion**. Energy is released. Carbon dioxide and water are formed, along with other unwanted substances.

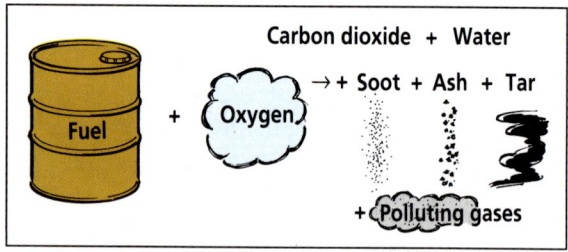

8 **Pollution** is the contamination of the environment by substances made by humans. Combustion of fuels often causes air pollution.

Pollution must be cut down, and this costs money. We have to balance this cost against the benefits of controlling pollution.

9 Many fuels, particularly coal and coke, contain sulphur. When they burn, the acidic gas sulphur dioxide is formed. This can help form **acid rain**.

Acid rain is harmful to living things such as trees and life in rivers and lakes. Acid rain and sulphur dioxide in the air cause damage to buildings. They make metals corrode faster.

10 Most of the sulphur dioxide can be removed from power station flue gases by a **flue-gas desulphurization** (**FGD**) plant, but this is expensive to install and run. It requires large amounts of limestone and produces large quantities of gypsum.

IN BRIEF: ENERGY TODAY AND TOMORROW

11 A **nuclear fuel** contains atoms with large, unstable nuclei. If a neutron hits one of these nuclei, the nucleus splits in half, releasing energy. This splitting is called **fission**. Several neutrons are also emitted, which can cause other fissions. This may lead to a **chain reaction** in which large amounts of energy are released.

12 There are both benefits and drawbacks to nuclear power.

Benefits	Drawbacks
(a) Nuclear fuels will last for another 2000 years.	(a) Nuclear power stations involve risks from accidents with radioactive substances.
(b) Nuclear fuels produce no smoke, no soot and no acid rain.	(b) There are dangers from leaks of radioactive substances from nuclear power stations.
(c) Unlike fossil-fuelled power stations, nuclear power stations do not emit carbon dioxide. The amount of this gas in the atmosphere is increasing, and this may be causing global warming.	(c) Some of the waste from nuclear reactors will be radioactive for hundreds of years and is extremely difficult to dispose of safely.
(d) Nuclear fuel saves valuable fossil fuels for other uses.	

13 Renewable energy sources will last as long as the Earth itself. Their supply is unlimited.

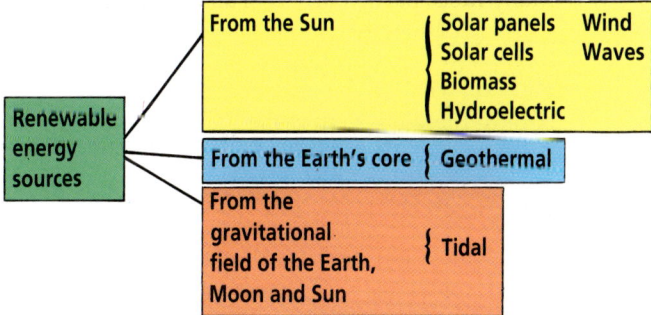

14 Renewable energy sources are difficult to **harness**. Their energy is very 'spread out' or dispersed. It is difficult to concentrate this energy to produce high temperatures or to generate electricity.

15 Nuclear fusion may be the energy source of the future. When two small nuclei of light elements are joined together (fused), energy is released. Fusion reactions inside the Sun provide the Sun's energy but they are proving very difficult to harness on Earth.

16 A **transformer** is used to change the voltage of an electricity supply. It consists of two separate coils wound on the same iron core. When the current changes in one coil (the **primary**) it induces a current in the other coil (the **secondary**). An alternating current in the primary induces another alternating current in the secondary.

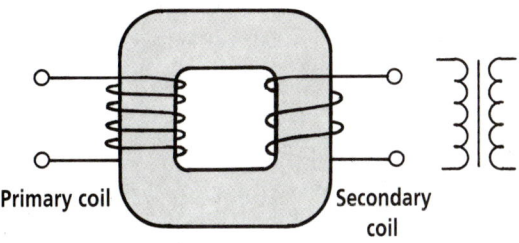

Primary coil   Secondary coil

The secondary voltage can be calculated from the equation:

$$\frac{\text{secondary voltage}}{\text{primary voltage}} = \frac{\text{number of turns in secondary coil}}{\text{number of turns in primary coil}}$$

or voltage ratio = turns ratio

17 If the secondary has more turns than the primary, the transformer is a **step-up** transformer. If the secondary has fewer turns, it is a **step-down** transformer.

18 In a step-up transformer, the output (secondary) voltage is larger than the input. But the output *current* is lower than the input current – by the same ratio. This means that the input and output power is the same (as $P=IV$) – in a 'perfect' transformer. In a real transformer, there is some loss of power.

19 The National Grid is a network of cables and wires which links all the power stations in Britain to the users of electricity. Transformers step up the voltage from the power stations to over 400 000 V for long-distance transmission. This means that the current in the cables is low and less energy is lost in transmission.

Thinking about

Energy Today and Tomorrow

1. What do we use fuels for?

In the UK, we use 8 000 000 000 000 MJ (8 million million megajoules) of energy in one year. On average that comes to almost 150 000 MJ for each person in the country – equivalent to 5.4 tonnes of coal, or 3.3 tonnes of oil, or 3800 cubic metres of gas used up in a year by each one of us.

The fuels we use in the UK
The pie charts below show how much of each type of fuel we use in the UK.

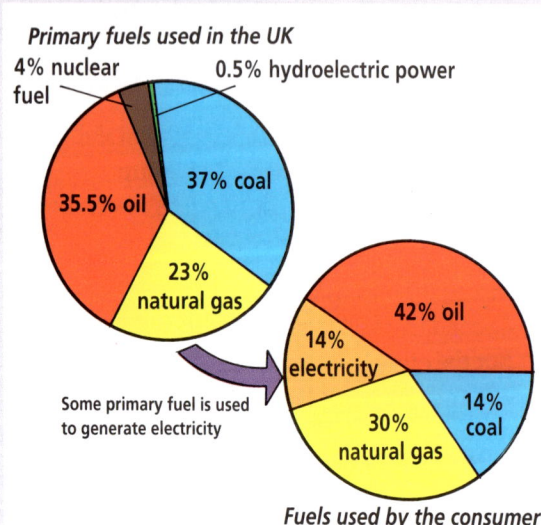

Primary fuels used in the UK
4% nuclear fuel
0.5% hydroelectric power
37% coal
35.5% oil
23% natural gas

Some primary fuel is used to generate electricity

42% oil
14% electricity
30% natural gas
14% coal

Fuels used by the consumer

Notice the difference between these two pie charts. The first shows the **primary** fuels. Some of these are used to generate electricity, which is then supplied to factories, offices and homes. The second pie chart shows the form in which the fuel reaches the consumer.

The fuels we use at home
If we look just at the fuels used in people's homes, the pattern is slightly different. Can you think of reasons for these differences?

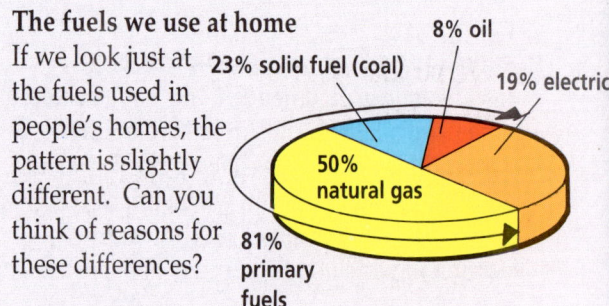

8% oil
23% solid fuel (coal)
19% electricity
50% natural gas
81% primary fuels

The table below summarizes the advantages and disadvantages of the four main fuels.

Fuel	Cost per MJ (pence)	Advantages	Disadvantages
Coal	0.40	Cheap Coal fires look nice	Dirty Difficult to transport Makes a lot of smoke and ash Difficult to light Risk of fires from sparks
Oil	0.48	Can be pumped automatically Clean to use No ash or smoke	Needs to be delivered every so often Messy and smelly if it leaks Price liable to vary more than other fuels
Gas	0.38	Doesn't need to be delivered Supply always available Very clean to use No ash or smoke	Supply has to be laid to the house Dangerous if it leaks
Electricity	1.38	Easy and quick to switch on and off Doesn't need to be delivered Very clean in use	Cables have to be laid to the house Danger of electric shocks Electrical faults can cause fires Waste produced at power stations

How we use fuel
Almost three-quarters of the fuel we use at home is for keeping the house warm (space heating) and for heating water. We can choose which fuel to use for this. We can also choose the fuel we prefer for cooking. But the 10% share for lighting and domestic appliances is almost all supplied by electricity.

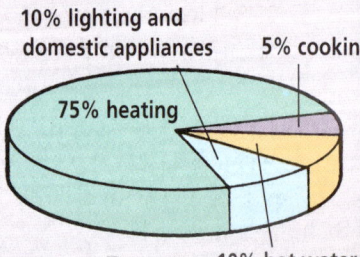

10% lighting and domestic appliances
5% cooking
75% heating
10% hot water

2. How do we make electricity?

A tiny amount of the electricity we use comes from batteries, but all the rest comes from the mains supply. It is generated using a method discovered by Michael Faraday in the 1830s, called **electromagnetic induction**.

Faraday found that he could generate a pulse of current in a circuit by moving a wire through the magnetic field between two magnets.

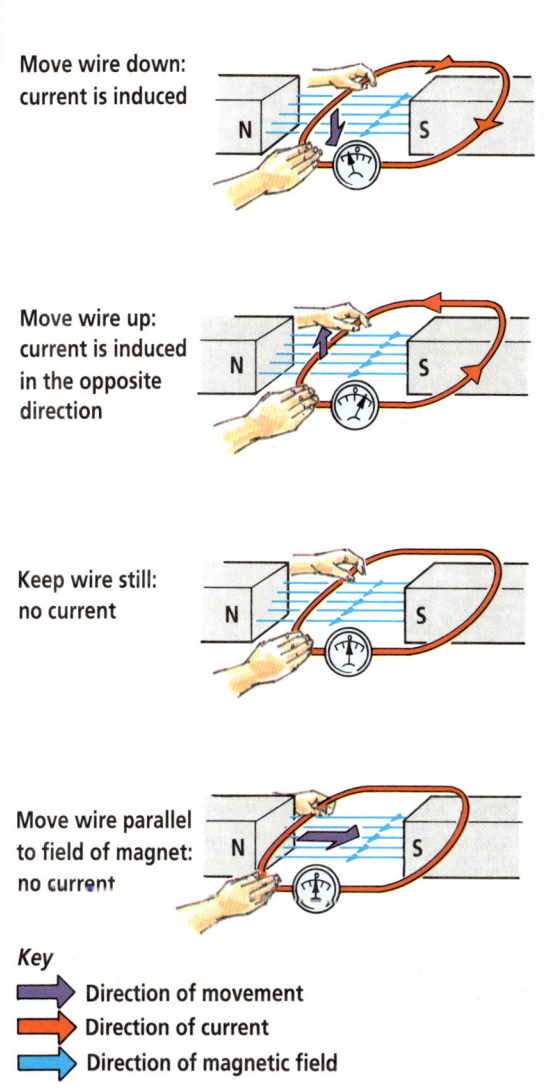

Key
- Direction of movement
- Direction of current
- Direction of magnetic field

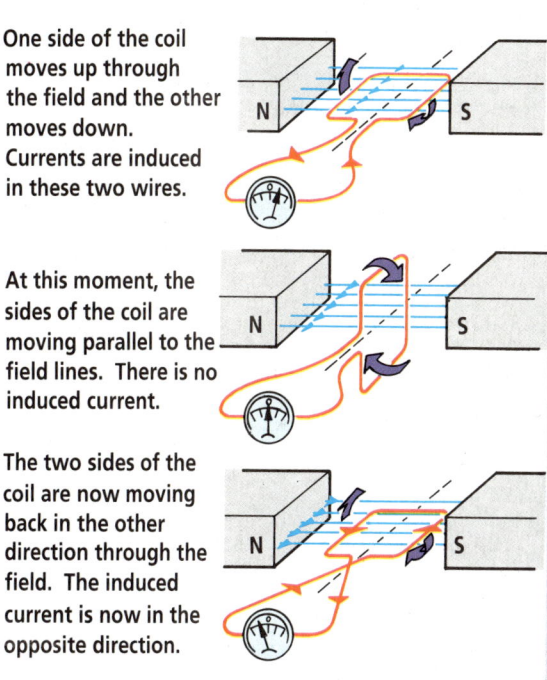

One side of the coil moves up through the field and the other moves down. Currents are induced in these two wires.

At this moment, the sides of the coil are moving parallel to the field lines. There is no induced current.

The two sides of the coil are now moving back in the other direction through the field. The induced current is now in the opposite direction.

As the coil rotates, an electric current is induced in it. This current keeps changing direction – it is an **alternating current**. In the simple design above, there is an obvious problem – the wires to the coil become twisted. This is solved by using two slip rings with brushes to make the electrical connections to the coil.

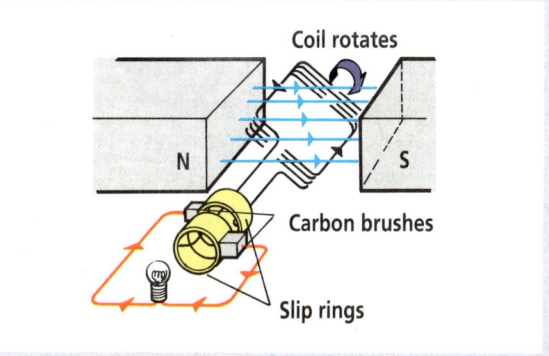

For a continuous supply of electricity, you need continuous movement of the wire. So to make a **generator**, you rotate a flat coil between the magnets.

You can make the current bigger by:
- using stronger magnets
- winding the coil on a soft-iron core to increase the magnetic field strength (as in an electromagnet)
- using a coil with more turns
- turning the coil faster.

If you turn the coil faster, the **frequency** of the alternating current will also increase.

3. How does a power station work?

A power station is a factory for generating electricity. Its raw material is a **primary fuel**. The large power station in the photo uses **coal** as its primary fuel. You can see the coal storage area at the front of the photo. The heart of the station is the square building in the middle. This contains the **turbines** and **generators**, and the **furnaces** which burn the coal. A large power station like this will have four generators, each with its own turbine.

Coal travels up a conveyor belt (shown in the photo) and into the power station. Here it is ground into powder and then blown into the furnaces. The powdered coal burns very quickly and produces a high temperature. This turns water in the boilers into steam. By keeping the pressure high, the steam is heated to over 800°C.

The high-pressure steam is then used to turn the turbines. Turbines are like specially designed windmills. A large number of thin blades are connected like spokes to an axle. You can see the turbine blades at the top of the photo on the opposite page. The steam hits these blades from one side. As it passes through the gaps, it makes the blades and axle spin. The spinning turbine shaft is used to turn the moving coil, or **rotor**, of a generator, producing electricity.

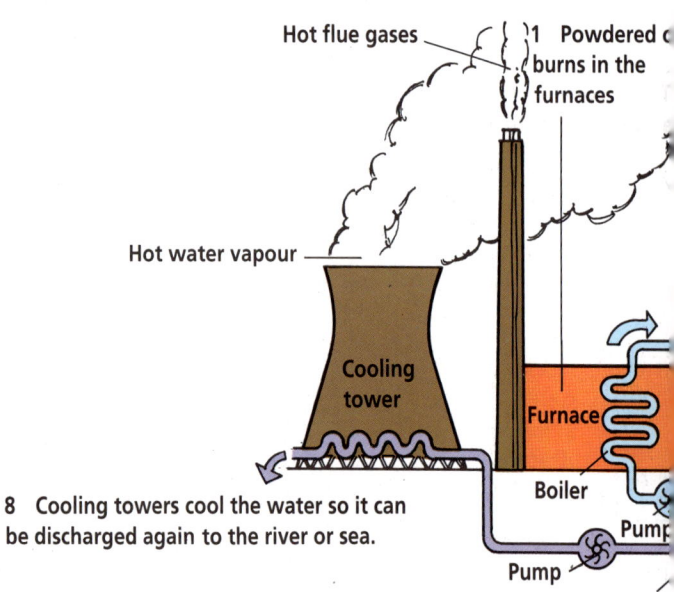

8 Cooling towers cool the water so it can be discharged again to the river or sea.

7 Low-pressure steam is recycled

How efficient is a power station?

How much of the energy released when the coal is burnt is transferred to the electricity?

Some energy is carried away by the hot flue gases from the furnaces. This goes up the chimneys and is wasted. The most important energy loss, however, is in the turbines. Once the steam has passed through the blades it is cooled, to reduce its pressure and make it condense. This **pressure difference** between the steam entering the turbine and the steam leaving it is what makes the turbine turn.

The steam is cooled by water, usually taken from a nearby river. This cooling water gets hot as a result and is piped away to large cooling towers to cool down before it goes back into the river. The white fumes you see around the tops of cooling towers are steam (from the hot cooling water), not smoke.

Because of these energy losses, a power station is around 35% efficient. This is not because it has been badly designed. There is a limit to the maximum efficiency possible.

Energy stored in coal and oxygen mixture (100 units)
- Energy in hot waste gases from chimney (15 units)
- Energy in hot high-pressure steam
  - Energy in heating of moving parts due to friction (5 units)
  - Energy carried away by cooling water (45 units)
  - Energy supplied as electricity (35 units)

THINKING ABOUT: ENERGY TODAY AND TOMORROW

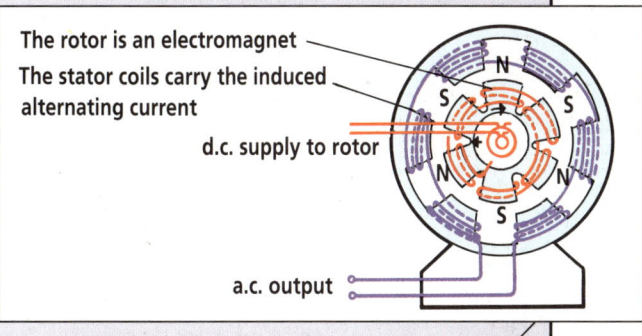

The rotor is an electromagnet
The stator coils carry the induced alternating current
d.c. supply to rotor
a.c. output

How does the generator work?

A power station generator is similar in design to the simple generator described on page 77. However, it produces very large currents. The simple generator uses brushes to take the current from the coil. There is always some sparking at brushes and with large currents these sparks would be very large. So the magnet is rotated rather than the coil. The coil (called the **stator**) is wound on a fixed iron frame, with a rotating electromagnet (the **rotor**) in the middle. The current to the electromagnet has to be supplied using brushes, but this current is quite small. As the rotor spins, it induces an alternating current in the stator coil. The electrons move to and fro.

This produces high-pressure steam at 800°C in the boilers.

4 The turbines turn the rotor inside the stator. This produces electricity in the generator.

This turns the turbines.

Rotor
Stator
Generator

5 The step-up transformer raises the voltage and the electricity enters the National Grid.

6 Cooling water from the river or sea cools the steam after it has turned the turbines.

What happens after the generators?

The generators are carefully controlled to spin at exactly 50 turns per second. This generates alternating current with a frequency of 50 Hz. Step-up transformers raise the voltage to over 400 000 V for long-distance transmission through the National Grid (see *Looking At The National Grid* on pages 72–3).

From the National Grid to your home

The cables in the National Grid carry the alternating current to your home. Wires from the cables are connected through various circuits to the live and neutral wires in the sockets. When you plug in an appliance such as a kettle you complete the circuit and a current flows through the appliance.

Are other types of power station the same?

Some power stations burn **oil** or **natural gas**, instead of coal. These are almost the same as a coal-fired power station. The only difference is in the design of the boiler.

Nuclear power stations are also very similar (see page 81). A nuclear reaction produces high-pressure steam. This then drives turbines and generators in the same way. A nuclear reactor just boils water in a different way.

Hydroelectric stations also have turbines, but these are driven directly by water, not by steam (see page 83). The water turbines then drive the generators.

In this photograph, the turbine (top) and two generators are open for maintenance and repair. Notice how big they are compared with the workers.

4. How do we use nuclear power?

Hartlepool nuclear power station can generate enough electricity to supply a large city. Notice there is no chimney. Its primary fuel is the nuclear fuel **uranium**. The power station needs much less fuel than a coal-fired station and produces much less waste. However, the fuel is much more expensive to produce and must be handled with great care, and the waste is much more difficult to deal with.

How does a nuclear power station work?

Nuclear fission

Uranium is a metal which occurs naturally in various ores. 99.3% of natural uranium is the isotope uranium-238; the other 0.7% is uranium-235. Both isotopes are radioactive – they are alpha emitters.

Uranium-235 has another property which was first discovered in 1938 by a team of German scientists, led by Lise Meitner and Otto Hahn. If a nucleus of uranium-235 is hit by a neutron, it splits into two roughly equal parts, shooting out a few more neutrons in the process. This is called **fission**.

The extra neutrons emitted can then strike other uranium-235 nuclei, causing them to split too. Very rapidly the fission spreads throughout the uranium sample – a **chain reaction** starts.

When each uranium nucleus splits, a small amount of energy is released. This is mainly kinetic energy at first, as the bits of the uranium nucleus fly off at very high speeds. As they go, they collide with other atoms, making them vibrate. The result is that everything gets very hot.

If there is only a small piece of uranium-235, most of the neutrons produced escape from the sample and the chain reaction stops. In a larger piece, an uncontrolled chain reaction will lead to an explosion. This is how nuclear weapons work.

In a nuclear reactor the chain reaction is controlled, giving a steady heat output.

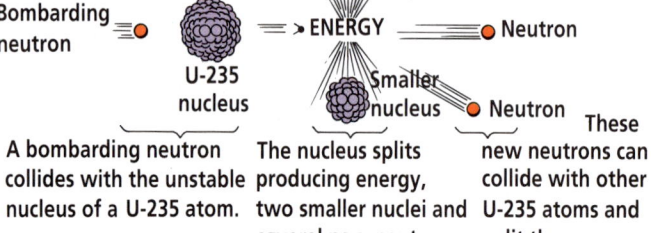

Fission – splitting an atom of uranium-235

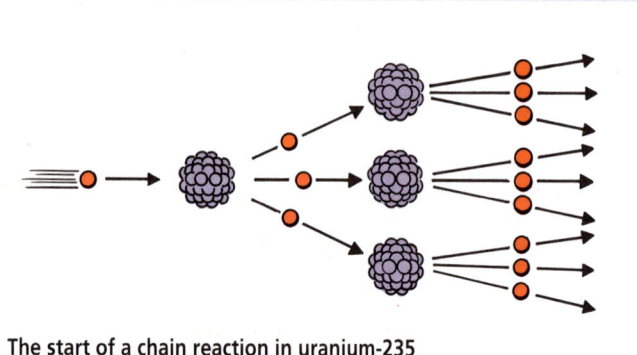

The start of a chain reaction in uranium-235

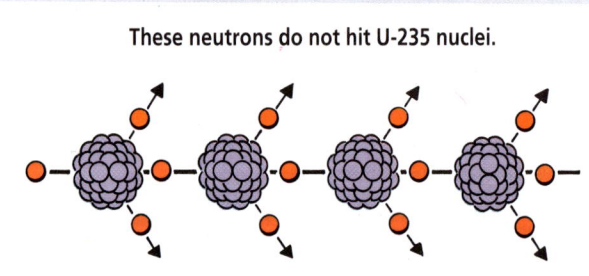

A controlled chain reaction

Nuclear reactors

The diagram shows an advanced gas-cooled reactor like the one in Hartlepool power station.

Fuel: The fuel is **enriched uranium oxide**. 'Enriched' means that some of the uranium-238 has been removed from the natural uranium, so that the proportion of uranium-235 is now around 2%. Pellets of enriched uranium oxide are loaded into steel tubes called **fuel pins**. The pins are arranged side by side in large steel cylinders called **fuel elements**.

Core: The fuel elements slot into holes in a **graphite core**. Graphite (a form of carbon) is a **moderator**. It slows down the fast neutrons from the fission process, so that they can be more easily absorbed by other uranium nuclei, causing more fissions.

Control rods: These can be raised or lowered to change the rate of the chain reaction. The rods are made of boron, a light metal which is good at absorbing neutrons.

Coolant: Carbon dioxide is circulated through the reactor. It heats up, carrying away the energy from the chain reaction and keeping the reactor cool. The hot carbon dioxide is used to boil water and produce high-pressure steam. This then drives the turbines (as in a coal-fired power station, pages 78-9).

Pressure vessel and shielding: The reactor sits inside a stainless steel pressure vessel which holds the high-pressure coolant gas. This is all surrounded by concrete shielding, which absorbs the radiation from the radioactive substances in the reactor and provides an extra safeguard against the high temperatures and pressures inside.

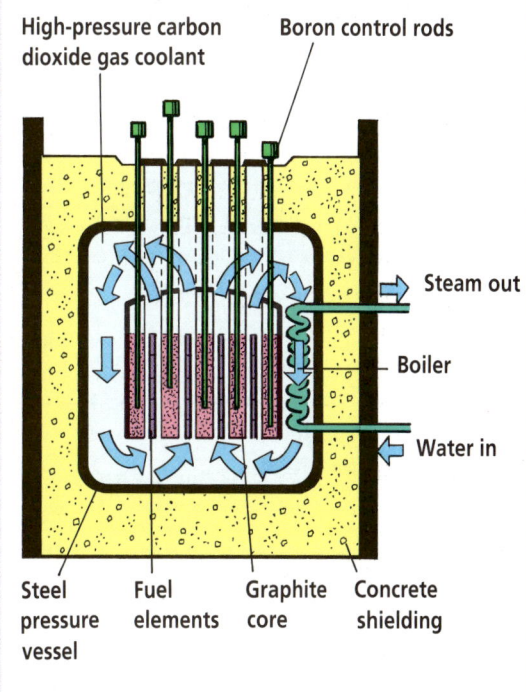

Fitting the fuel pins into a fuel element

Loading fuel elements into the reactor core

Pressurized water reactors (PWRs)

Some of the newer nuclear power stations in Britain are PWRs. In this design, water acts as both the coolant and the moderator. The hot water leaving the reactor vessel is at several hundred degrees Celsius. But it is under very high pressure so that it cannot boil and turn to steam. It is used to boil water in another separate circuit, which then drives the turbines.

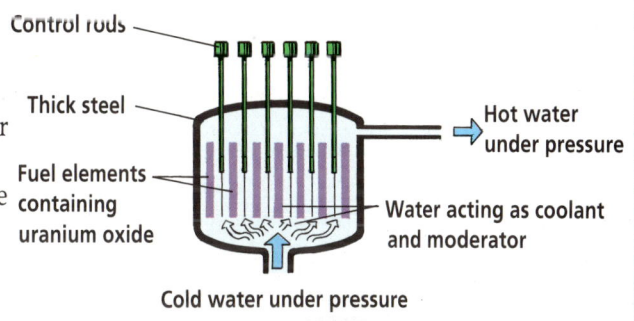

5. What are renewable energy sources?

Limited reserves

If we keep on using oil at the present rate, the world's supplies will run out before the year 2050. Coal will last a little longer, but it too will be all used up within about 300 years. There is only a limited amount of uranium ore in the Earth's crust, so nuclear fuel will also run out. What alternatives are there? Many people think that we should be putting more effort into developing the **renewable** energy sources – sources which will last as long as the Earth itself.

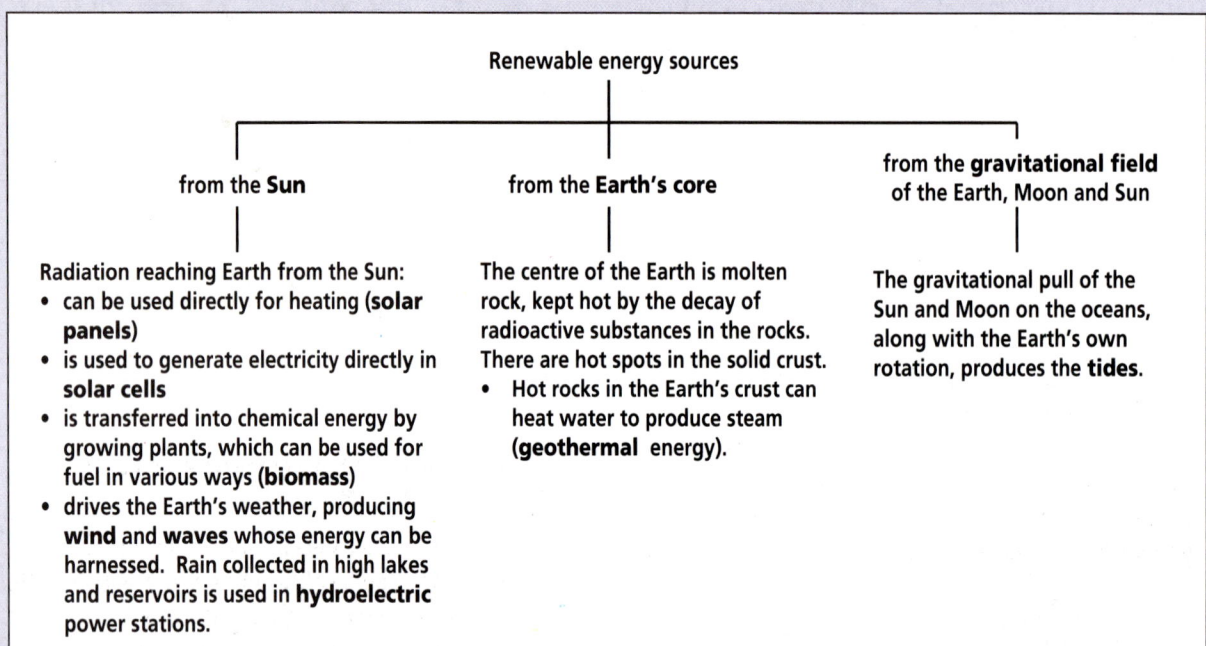

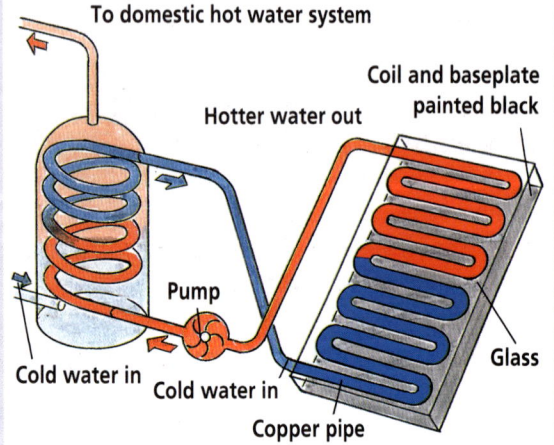

Solar panels

Solar panels on a south-facing roof help to provide hot water for a house. They work best on sunny, cloudless days. When it is cloudy, the panels still partially heat the water, so that less fossil fuel is needed to heat it to the required temperature.
A simple solar panel consists of a coil of copper pipe mounted on a metal baseplate. This is painted black to absorb the Sun's radiation. The glass cover allows the short wavelength infra-red radiation from the Sun to pass through. The hot panel emits longer wavelength infra-red radiation which cannot pass back out through the glass – the 'greenhouse effect'. The hot water from the panel is used to heat the domestic hot water and is then recycled through the panel again.

Solar cells

A **solar cell** is made from a very thin sandwich of semiconductor materials. It becomes like a little battery, with a voltage across its terminals, when light shines on it. Modern solar cells can convert about 15% of the light energy they receive into electrical energy.

It takes quite a lot of energy to make a solar cell. But once it is made it has a long working lifetime. It has no moving parts and needs no maintenance.

THINKING ABOUT: ENERGY TODAY AND TOMORROW

Biomass

One of the most efficient ways of trapping the Sun's energy is by growing plants. Taking the Earth as a whole, energy is being trapped by the growth of new plant matter six times faster than we are using up energy in fossil fuels.

In Brazil sugar from sugar cane is fermented to produce alcohol. Engines can be modified to run on a mixture of petrol with 20% alcohol.

Wind energy

Windmills used to be used in many countries for grinding corn and pumping water. Today windmills are making a comeback – with modern designs. A modern **wind turbine** uses the kinetic energy of the wind to drive a turbine and generator to make electricity.

This 3 MW wind turbine on Orkney is part of the National Grid. It would take about 600 of these to generate as much electricity as a coal-fired power station.

Wave power

Waves carry an enormous amount of energy. The problem is how to make use of it. One idea is to use a line of nodding '**ducks**'. These would bob back and forth as the waves passed. Inside each duck is a small generator, driven by the motion of the duck. Cables then carry the electricity back to land.

The back and forth motion of the duck can be used to generate electricity.

The line of ducks could be several hundred metres long. It has to be flexible enough to move with the waves, yet strong enough to withstand heavy seas. Britain's first wave power station, using a different, shoreline based design, was opened on the Island of Islay on 15 July 1991.

Hydroelectric energy

About 0.5% of our electricity in the UK is generated by **hydroelectric** power stations. In some countries like Norway and Canada the proportion is much larger. Water from a river or a storage dam is used to drive large water turbines. These then turn generators to produce electricity.

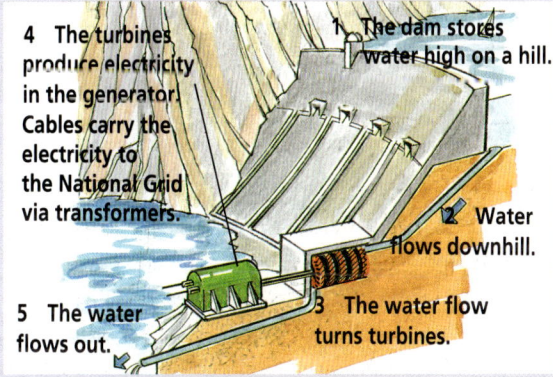

1. The dam stores water high on a hill.
2. Water flows downhill.
3. The water flow turns turbines.
4. The turbines produce electricity in the generator. Cables carry the electricity to the National Grid via transformers.
5. The water flows out.

Geothermal energy

Reykjavik, the capital of Iceland, has a lower average temperature than any town in Britain. Yet the inhabitants can keep warm without burning any fossil fuel at all. Iceland is a volcanic region and its capital is heated by natural hot water springs – central heating without burning fuel.

Even where there are no natural hot springs, there are often hot rocks under the Earth's surface.

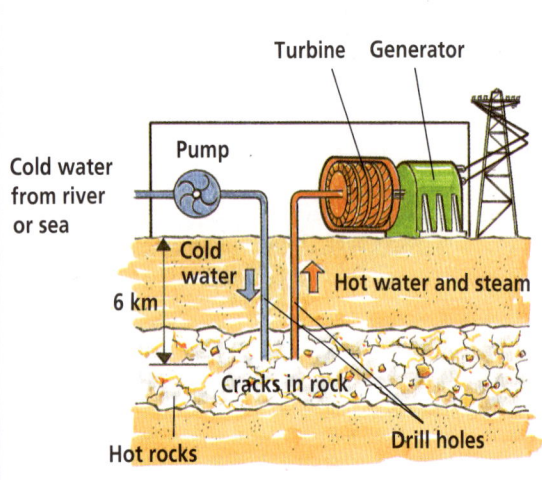

In a geothermal power station, cold water is pumped down to the hot rocks. It seeps through cracks, getting heated up in the process. The hot water comes up a second pipe to the surface where it boils, as the pressure on it is reduced. The steam can be used to drive a turbine and generator.

Tidal energy

To harness the power of the **tides**, a barrier is built across a river estuary. As the tide comes in, the water level outside the barrier is higher than inside. The water flows through turbines in the barrier, generating electricity as it goes.

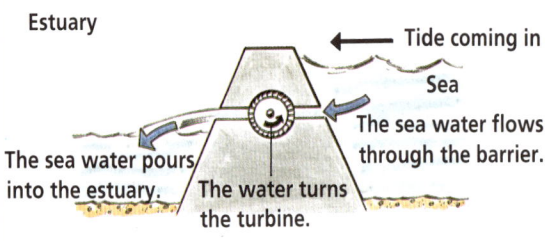

When the tide is out, the water level is higher in the estuary than in the sea. Water can pass through the turbines again as it flows out to the sea.

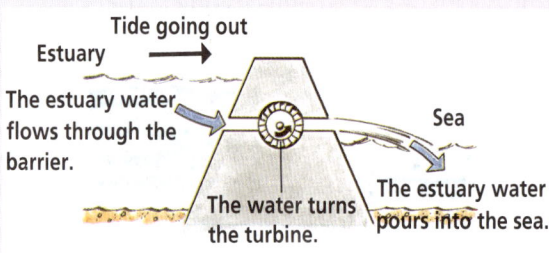

This tidal power station at La Rance in Brittany, France has been working since 1966. A road across the estuary runs along the top of the barrier.

Renewable energy – what's the problem?

Renewable energy sources seem an obvious and sensible alternative to fossil fuels. The energy is free and won't run out. There is no air pollution. So why do we use fossil fuels and nuclear fuel at all? The answer is that renewable energy sources are hard to **harness**. The energy of the wind and waves is very 'spread out', or **dispersed** – it is hard to collect. Solar and geothermal sources can produce low temperature heating for buildings but it is hard to get high enough temperatures to generate electricity. Tidal and hydroelectric schemes are large and expensive to set up. Although they do not pollute the air they have other environmental consequences.

6. Nuclear fusion – unlimited energy for the future?

Some people see **nuclear fusion** as our best hope for energy in the future. In nuclear **fission** (see page 80), a large nucleus (uranium) splits in half, releasing energy. Fusion is completely different: two very small and light nuclei (hydrogen or helium) are joined (**fused**) together to form a larger nucleus. This also releases energy. One possible nuclear fusion reaction is:

$${}^{2}_{1}H + {}^{3}_{1}H \rightarrow {}^{4}_{2}H + {}^{1}_{0}n$$

deuterium + tritium → helium + 1 neutron

Deuterium and tritium are two isotopes of hydrogen.

Research has been going on for many years but no one has yet managed to obtain more energy from a fusion reaction than that needed to set up the reaction in the first place. The problem is that nuclei are positively charged and repel each other. The atoms have to lose their electrons and become a **plasma** before the fusion reaction can begin. This needs very high temperatures, as much as 100 000 000 K.

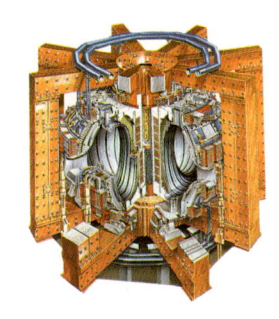

In the JET (Joint European Torus) project, a doughnut-shaped magnetic field is used to hold the hot plasma. The apparatus in the diagram is large – as high as a two-storey building.

In November 1991, JET project scientists reported that they had succeeded in controlling a fusion reaction for a short time.

Research continues because, if we could get it to work reliably on a large scale, the rewards would be enormous. The fuel is hydrogen. Water contains hydrogen and there is plenty of water around. And the products may not be as dangerously radioactive as waste from fission reactors.

The Sun's energy comes from fusion reactions inside the Sun. Perhaps solar energy is the only way we will ever succeed in making use of nuclear fusion.

7. How can we change voltages?

Thinking About 2 on page 77 explains how you can generate a pulse of current by moving a wire through a magnetic field. Another way to generate a current pulse is to plunge a bar magnet into a coil.

There is a brief pulse of current as the magnet moves into the coil. There is another pulse, in the opposite direction, when you pull the magnet out again.

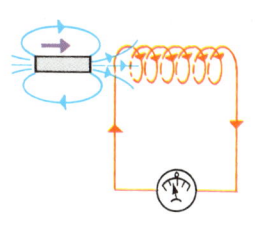

This also works if you use an electromagnet instead of a bar magnet. Now there is no need for anything to move. The magnetic field around the coil can be changed by simply switching the electromagnet on and off.

When you switch the electromagnet on, there is a brief pulse of current in the secondary circuit.

When you switch the electromagnet off again, there is another brief pulse of current in the opposite direction.

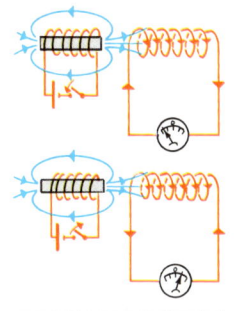

Current is induced in the secondary circuit when the current is *changing* in the primary circuit. An **alternating current** is always changing in size and direction. If we use an alternating current in the primary circuit, it induces another alternating current in the secondary circuit. This is how a **transformer** works.

In a transformer, both coils are wound on the same iron core, so that changes in the magnetic field of the primary coil are efficiently carried to the secondary coil.

Notice that the primary and secondary coils are completely insulated from one another. They are linked only by the changing magnetic field in the core.

The transformer rule

There is a very simple rule for predicting the output (secondary) voltage of a transformer.

voltage ratio = turns ratio

$$\frac{\text{secondary voltage}}{\text{primary voltage}} = \frac{\text{number of turns on secondary}}{\text{number of turns on primary}}$$

In symbols, this is written

$$\frac{V_s}{V_p} = \frac{N_s}{N_p}$$

If a transformer has more turns in its secondary coil, then the output (secondary) voltage is bigger than the input (primary) voltage. This is called a **step-up** transformer. If there are fewer turns in the secondary, the output (secondary) voltage is smaller than the input (primary) voltage. This is a **step-down** transformer.

But where does the extra voltage come from in a step-up transformer, and where does it go in a step-down transformer? In a step-up transformer, the *current* in the secondary coil is *smaller* than the current in the primary. For example, if the output voltage is twice the input voltage, then the output current will be half the input current. The *power* is the same in both coils in an ideal transformer. (Remember: power = current × voltage; $P = IV$.)

Transformers are used in all mains/battery appliances. This radio can work from the mains or from six 1.5 V cells. It contains a transformer to step down the mains voltage to near 9 V. Other circuits then convert the low voltage a.c. to d.c. and stabilize it at exactly 9 V.

Transformers in the National Grid

Looking At The National Grid on pages 72-3 explains how electricity is distributed from power stations to users. Transformers are used to step up the voltage to 275 000 V or 400 000 V for long-distance transmission. The voltage is then stepped down again to 240 V nearer the consumer. What are the advantages of high voltage transmission and why are such high voltages used?

The best way to answer these questions is by an example. Imagine that we have to supply 10 kW from a power station to a consumer. The resistance of the long cables required is 10 Ω.

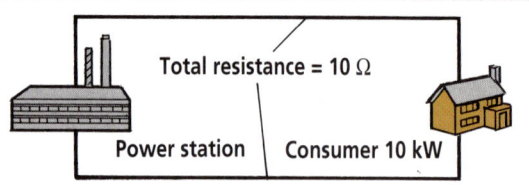

Method 1: low voltage transmission

We supply the 10 kW by transmitting at 100 V. The current is 100 A (using $P = IV$). Substituting Ohm's law, $V = IR$, in $P = IV$, gives $P = I^2R$

Power lost in the cables = I^2R
  = $(100)^2 \times 10$ W
  = 100 000 W = 100 kW

To get 10 kW to the consumer, we have to supply 110 kW. 100 kW are wasted heating up the cables.

Method 2: high voltage transmission

We supply the 10 kW by transmitting at 100 000 V. The current is now 0.1 A.

Power lost in the cables = I^2R
  = $(0.1)^2 \times 10$ W
  = 0.1 W

To get 10 kW (10 000 W) to the consumer, we have to supply 10 000.1 W. Only 0.1 W is wasted in the cables.

High-voltage transmission means that the current in the cables is much smaller. So thinner cables can be used and much less energy is lost in heating the cables.

Things to do

Energy Today and Tomorrow

Things to try out

1 Were they the good old days? For this activity you will need to talk to someone who is over 70 years old.

Ask them what things were like when they were your age. Ask them:
(a) What fuel was used to warm their home?
(b) Was every room heated? If not, which rooms were heated?
(c) Did they have hot running water? If not, how did they heat water when they needed it?
(d) What fuel was used for cooking food?
(e) What means of transport did they use
  (i) for journeys of less than 2 miles or so
  (ii) for journeys of over 2 miles or so?

2 Design a questionnaire that you could use with the students in your class to find out which fuels are used to heat their homes and for cooking food. Also include a question to find out what forms of insulation are used in their houses. Use the questionnaire to collect information from several classes. Present your findings in tables and bar charts.

Things to find out

3 In some parts of the world, geothermal energy is used for heating homes. Use the school library or the local public library to find out as much as you can about the use of geothermal energy in Iceland or in New Zealand.

4 In April 1989, two scientists, Martin Fleischmann and Stanley Pons, startled the scientific world by announcing that they had managed to produce a nuclear fusion reaction at room temperature in a test tube – cold fusion. Many articles about it appeared in newspapers and in journals like the *New Scientist* during April and May 1989. Find out as much as you can about the cold fusion story:
- what did the scientists say they had found?
- how did they claim to have done it?
- why did the report cause such a stir?
- how did other scientists respond?

Things to write about

5 The diagram shows a bicycle dynamo. Read the section on generators on page 77 and use it to write an explanation of how the dynamo works.

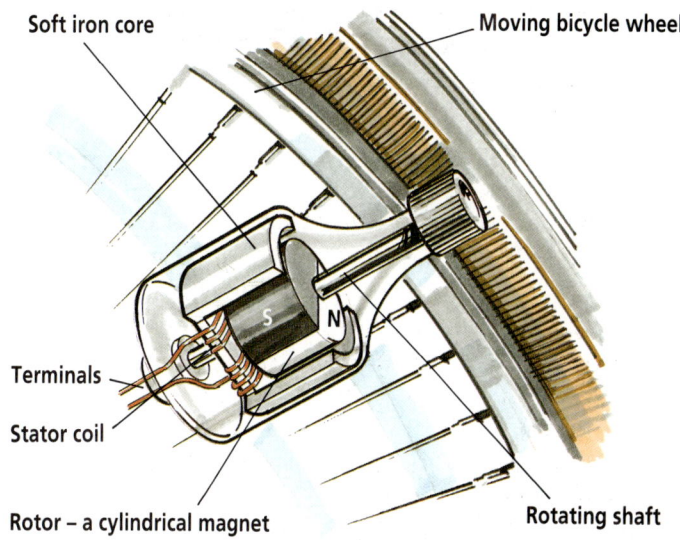

6 (a) Explain what is meant by the term 'renewable energy source'.
(b) A magazine article about energy contains this passage:

> One of the difficulties with renewable energy sources is that the energy is very 'spread out'. It is very difficult to use them to produce a 'concentrated' form of energy like electricity.

Explain what you think this means and give some examples to show how some of the renewable energy sources are 'spread out'.

Points to discuss

7 Look at the table on page 76 showing the costs, advantages and disadvantages of different fuels. Which fuel would be best for each of the following? Give a reasons for each choice.
(a) fuelling a power station in Yorkshire
(b) fuelling a power station in Saudi Arabia
(c) heating an oven in a large bakery
(d) heating steel bars in a steelworks before rolling them to make a steel plate
(e) heating a large greenhouse used for growing tomatoes

Questions to answer

8 The table below shows the amount of oil left and the amount being used each year in different parts of the world.

	Amount of oil left (million tonnes)	Amount being used up each year at present (million tonnes)
America	18 400	800
Europe	3640	140
Middle East	61 000	610
Africa	9460	220

(a) How long will oil last in the four parts of the world listed in the table? (Assume that it will continue to be used up at the same rate and none is exported.)
(b) Where is it likely that
  (i) oil will last the longest
  (ii) oil will be used up first?
(c) What are the major uses of oil?

9 Read carefully pages 80–81 on nuclear power. Then answer the following:
(a) Explain what is meant by nuclear fission.
(b) Nuclear reactors use uranium as fuel. Give two ways in which uranium fuel differs from conventional fuels such as coal or oil.
(c) If the control rods were raised a little (pulling them out of the reactor), what would be the effect on the fission reaction? Explain you answer.
(d) Why is the reactor enclosed in a thick concrete shield?
(e) Explain how heat released by the reactor is used to generate electricity.
(f) Some people argue that the UK should have more nuclear energy. Others argue that nuclear power should not be used at all. Give *two* arguments **(i)** in favour and **(ii)** against nuclear power.

10 Draw up a large table of information about renewable energy sources. Use the information on pages 82–4 to complete the table. Here are some headings you might include in your table:
- advantages
- disadvantages
- is it used to generate electricity?
- small scale or large scale source?
- cost to maintain (high, medium or low).

11 In the UK, on average, 20 W of solar energy arrives on each square metre of land during daylight hours. A solar power station is planned to produce 20 MW of electrical power. If the panels are 10% efficient (i.e. they transfer 10% of the solar energy into electrical energy), what area of solar panels is required?

12 What is the output voltage of these transformers (assuming they are 100% efficient)?

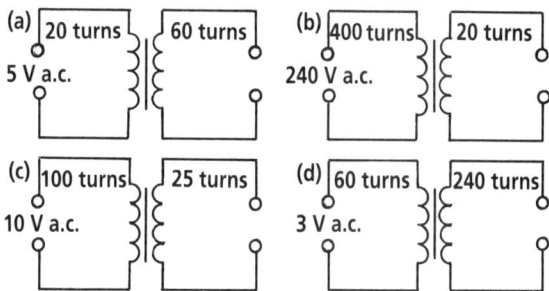

13 (a) A large coal-fired power station burns around 200 tonnes of coal in an hour. The main elements in coal are carbon, hydrogen and sulphur. 200 tonnes of typical coal might contain
- 144 tonnes of carbon
- 40 tonnes of hydrogen
- 3 tonnes of sulphur.

When the coal burns, these elements react with oxygen:

$$\text{carbon} + \text{oxygen} \rightarrow \text{carbon dioxide}$$
$$C(s) + O_2(g) \rightarrow CO_2(g)$$

$$\text{hydrogen} + \text{oxygen} \rightarrow \text{water vapour}$$
$$2H_2(g) + O_2(g) \rightarrow 2H_2O(g)$$

$$\text{sulphur} + \text{oxygen} \rightarrow \text{sulphur dioxide}$$
$$S(s) + O_2(g) \rightarrow SO_2(g)$$

The relative atomic masses of these elements are as follows: hydrogen, 1; carbon, 12; oxygen, 16; sulphur, 32. Use the equations to work out how many tonnes of carbon dioxide, water vapour and sulphur dioxide you would get from 200 tonnes of coal. In addition, you would have around 13 tonnes of ash (the part of the coal that does not burn).

(b) Copy the matter flow diagram on page 70 and mark on it the masses of all materials entering and leaving the power station every hour.

Index

Acid rain 52,54,70,74
Acquired characteristics 27
Activation energy 54,57
AGR (advanced gas-cooled reactor) 81
Alkali metals 60
Alkanes 54
Alleles 26,27,29,30
   codominant 27,34
   dominant 27,29
   recessive 27,29
Alpha emitter 85
Alternating current 74,77,85,86
Amino acids, code for 32
Apollo 11 2
Artificial selection 19,26,28
Asteroid 6
Astronomy, radio 16
Atmosphere 8
Atom 55

Balance 39,44,45,46
Bases, in DNA 32
Battery 68
Biomass 82,83
Black hole 6,17
Bond 54
   breaking 57
   covalent 55,59,63
   ionic 55,58,63
   making 57
   metallic 64
Burning 49,56

Car engine 52
Carbon 64
Carbon dioxide 54,56
Carbon monoxide 52,54,56
Catalytic convertor 53,54
Cell division 29
Centre of mass 36,37,39,45
Chain reaction 75,80
Characteristics 26
Chlorine 61
Chromosomes 26,27,28,31
   and sexual reproduction 29
   sex 31

Circular motion 13
Clones 32
Coal 67,70,71,72,74
Co-dominance 27,34
Colour blindness 31,34
Combustion 74
Comet 6
Control rods 81
Core, reactor 81
Cross-pollination 24,25,34

Davy lamp 51
Deuterium 85
Diamond 64
Displacement reactions 61
DNA 27,31,32
Dominant allele 27
Double helix 27,31

Earth 1,2,4,10
Efficiency, of power station 78
Elbow joint 44
Electrochemistry 51
Electromagnetic induction 74,77,85
Electron 62
Elements 60
   discovery of 51
Energy 38,40
   dispersal 74,84
   flow 70
   reserves 67
   sources, renewable 67,75,82,83,84
Environmental factors affecting variation 26,28
Evolution 19,20,21,26,28
Exothermic reaction 54,57

FGD (flue-gas desulphurization) 71,74
Fitness 35,41,46,47
Flashpoint 54
Force 39,40
   gravitational 7,13,14
Fosbury flop 35,36
Fossil fuels 67,74
Fossils 22,23
Fuels 54,56
   use of 74,76

Galapagos Islands 20
Galapagos finches 20

Galaxy	1
Gene cloning	27
Generator	77,78,79
Genes	26,28,29
Genetic code	31,32
Genetic engineering	27,32
Geological time	22
Geothermal energy	82,84
Glucose	38,42
Graphite	64
Gravitational field	7
Gravitational potential energy	36,38,39,41,42,43
Gravity	2,4,5,7,13
Greenhouse effect	52,54
Group	55,60,63
Gypsum	71,74
Haemophilia	34
Halogens	61
High jump	35,36
Homologous pairs of chromosomes	27,29
Hydrocarbons	52,54,56
Hydroelectric energy	79,82,83
Inertia	7
Inheritance, patterns of	30
Inherited factors	24,26
Ion	55,58
Inverter	69
JET (Joint European Torus) project	85
Joints	39,43,44
Joules	38
Jumping	36
Kinetic energy	36,37,38,39,40,42,43
Lactic acid	38,42
Lattice	
giant	55
molecular	55
Lead pollution	52,54
Lever	39,43,44
Mass	7,14,39
Matter flow	70
Methane	51,54,56
Method of science	17
Milky Way	1
Moderator	81
Molecule	55
Momentum	11
Moon	2,3,4,5
landing	2,3
Muscles	38,39,42,43
Mutations	27
National Grid	72,75,79,86
Natural selection	21,26,28
Nebula	6
Neptune, discovery of	16
Neutron star	6,17
Newton's laws	6,10,11
Newton metre	38
Nuclear	
fission	75,80
fuel	67,74,75
fusion	6,75,85
power	72,75,79,80
reactors	79,81
Observation	7,17,20
Orbit	2,6,7,10,12,13,15
Peas	24
Periodic table	55,60
Planet	1,6,8,9,15
Planets, data	8,9
Plasma	85
Plasmids	32
Pole vault	36,37
Pollution	52,54,70,71,74
Potential energy	36,38,41,42,43
Power	35,38,41
Power station	7
coal	70,72,78,79
hydroelectric	79,82,83
nuclear	72,75,79,80
oil	72,79
Prediction	7,17
Pressure vessel	81
Projectile	7,12
Pulsar	16
Pure-breeding	24
PWR (pressurized water reactor)	81
Radioactive	85
Recessive allele	27